The Ghosts of November

Memoirs of an Outsider Who Witnessed the Carnage at Jonestown, Guyana

by
Jeffrey Brailey

Published by: J & J Publishers, Post Office Box 240808, San Antonio, Texas 78224, USA

First printing November 1998

Front and back covers designed by
John Crain & Company / Graphic Design
520 Madison
San Antonio, Texas 78204
(210) 224-9751

Front cover photos courtesy John and Barbara Moore

"Last Rights" by Rebecca Moore first appeared in In Defense of the people's Temple and Other Essays, published by the Edwin Mellen Press, Lewiston, NY, 1988 and is used by permission of the author.

All of the information found in Chapter Six is taken from "With All Due Honors: A History of the Quartermaster Graves Registration Mission," an article by Dr. Steven E. Anders, MD, the historian of the U.S. Army Quartermaster Corps. The article appeared in the September 1988 issue of the Quartermaster Professional Bulletin.

Library of Congress Catalog Card Number: 98-88266

Brailey, Harold Jeffrey
The Ghosts of November: Memoirs of an Outsider Who Witnessed the Carnage at Jonestown, Guyana / by Jeffrey Brailey -- 1st ed.
Includes recommended readings and appendix
ISBN 0-9667868-0-7
1. Nonfiction / Horror
2. History - Military History
3. Guyana - Jonestown Tragedy

Dedication

To my wife Ann and my mother Carol, the two most important women in my life...

Table of Contents

Acknowledgements

This book would never had been written were it not for my wife and one true love, Jessie "Ann" Philips-Brailey. It was her positive guidance, unfailing patience, loving criticism and incessant prodding that caused **The Ghosts of November** to be written. The idea was entirely hers' and for that I am grateful.

The support and encouragement of Rebecca Moore and her husband Fielding McGehee had a profound influence on this book. This book would have been incomplete if she had not allowed me to include excerpts of her essay "Last Rights" in the Appendix. Her essay finally reveals for all to see how this tragedy ended.

The cover photos were contributed by John and Barbara Moore. It is through these photos taken of some of the ghosts of November before they perished, that they should be remembered; not as I saw them in death but as they lived their lives.

Dr. Steven E. Anders is the historian of the U.S. Army Quartermaster Corps. I owe most of Chapter Six to information I obtained from his article, "With All Due Honors: A History of the Graves Registration Mission," which appeared in the September 1988 issue of the **Quartermaster Professional Bulletin.**

Acknowledgements

The friendship, support and sharing of information with independent documentary producer Jim Hougan and director Steve Connolly of Channel 4 in Great Britain gave me the impetus to complete this book a week after our meeting in New York City. It was a privilege to be a part of their documentary on Jonestown.

Special thanks goes out to Rod Norberg, my editor, who spent countless hours checking my grammar, picking my brain and suggesting more descriptive words. His contribution to this book was invaluable.

Kevin Hozak's computer skills and technical expertise were greatly appreciated. Thanks for the e-mail, Kevin.

John Crain designed the front and back covers of **The Ghosts of November** . His artistic abilities are greatly appreciated and I hope we work on many more projects together.

Finally, my unending gratitude goes out to the men and women of the Joint Humanitarian Task Force to Guyana, without whom this book could not have been written. If what I have revealed opens old wounds or resurrects bad memories, forgive me. The Jonestown experience irrevocably changed everyone who was a part of it and I felt this story at last had to be told.

Prologue

Saturday, November 18, 1978 was a typical one for me. Twice a month, on the weekends following paydays, my wife and I would hit one of the casinos in Panama City, Panama. Each of us, armed with 20 dollars, would invade a popular gambling house in one of the city's hotels and play until the money ran out or we became too tired to play anymore. We rarely retreated in less than three hours and sometimes left victorious, with quite a bit more cash than we arrived with.

My then-wife, Mai, whom I met in Vietnam, once won 350 dollars; quite a feat for someone who only played the nickel slot machines, no more than three nickels at a time. My game was Blackjack and I attacked it with about as much ammunition as my ex-spouse did her slots. The two dollar tables were my battleground and two dollars was my permanent limit per hand.

As you read the first two paragraphs of this prologue, you might have wondered about the military terms that are sprinkled throughout them: armed, invade, retreated, victorious, attacked, ammunition and battleground. That may have something to do with my job from 1968 to 1988. I was a professional soldier.

From 1976 to 1980, I was stationed in Panama, assigned to the 601st Medical Company. The 601st was a clearing station, the closest medical unit to the front lines that has physicians, the capability to perform surgery and the ability to house injured and sick soldiers until they recover or can be evacuated to larger, more secure medical facilities.

The main mission of the 601st Medical Company in 1978 was to support the 193rd Infantry Brigade. This involved setting up medical treatment facilities during the field exercises the brigade's battalions regularly participated in. With three infantry battalions and part of a Special Forces Group to support, the 601st spent a great deal of time in the jungles of Panama.

Prologue

Occasionally, the soldiers of the 601st were given the opportunity to help the civilian population. This usually involved providing medical support to countries in Central and South America after a natural disaster. Sometimes we would send teams to Indian villages in remote jungle areas of Panama to help the Panamanian Defense Force medics treat the locals.

During the Vietnam War, these missions to the civilian community were called MedCAPs (Medical Civic Action Program). The soldiers of the 601st enjoyed going on MedCAPs. The missions gave them the opportunity to do something out of the ordinary, to help the local population and be able to interact with them, and to simply get away from the every day routine of soldiering. They also made the medics feel worthwhile because they were doing what they were trained to do, instead of playing war games. MedCAPs were useful and rewarding. They were, until Saturday, November 18, 1978.

Saturday evening, November 18, 1978, was not an untypical one for most of the residents of Jonestown, Guyana. They were responding to the call of their Messiah, Jim Jones, as they had dozens of times in the past when he shouted, "White Night, White Night, White

Night!" into the microphone that carried his forceful, charismatic voice throughout the enclave of freshly painted cottages the group of American expatriots had built in the jungle of Guyana.

Jones had time and time again warned his flock that the day would come when the American CIA would invade the sanctuary they had fashioned far from their homeland. Several times a month, the residents of Jonestown would respond to their leader's call to practice a form of ritual mass suicide he promised would result in their reincarnation. He also said that when they all returned, they would rule the world. His devout followers obeyed outrageous dictates as if they were in a hypnotic trance.

Sometimes, when Jones' followers partook of the fruity-tasting brew meant to take their lives, they would sleep for a while, but did not die. A sedative had been used during the rehearsals in place of the cyanide that Jones had standing by for the real show. Saturday, November 18, 1978, was not another dress rehearsal. Instead, it represented the final act of Jones' bizarre play.

It was the sole performance, played out by many unwilling, but mostly cooperative members of his huge cast.

The play was destined to open and close this night, the lives of the actors ended by the ingestion of a deadly poison instead of the sedative used during rehearsals. The play was to be remembered though; painfully remembered by those who knew the cast and would miss them; curiously remembered by those who became intrigued, puzzled and shocked when they learned of the action; and hauntingly remembered by those who cleaned up the theater after the final act. I was one of the latter.

> "Whatever you do you need courage. Whatever course you decide upon, there is always someone to tell you that you are wrong. There are always difficulties arising that tempt you to believe your critics are right. To map out a course of action and follow it to an end requires some of the same courage that a soldier needs. Peace has its victories, but it takes brave men and women to win them."
>
> **Ralph Waldo Emerson**

One

Life in the Tropics

Life in Panama was idyllic for the American soldiers of the 193rd Infantry Brigade and their families in the 1970's. Among old Canal Zone hands, Panama was known as the best kept secret in the Army. Military life is the same the world over, but the environment in which the duties of soldiers are performed makes all the difference in the world. Panama's temperature was always warm and in November 1978, the long rainy season was waning and the American residents of the Isthmus were eagerly awaiting Thanksgiving and Christmas. The holidays also signaled the commencement of the enjoyable but short dry season.

Field duty was always an adventure. The jungle was exotic and mysterious to Americans, even those who had spent several years in Panama. It was teeming with animal life that could only be viewed in zoos at home and the flora was equally unique. Many of us eagerly anticipated the frequent field exercises our unit participated in as opportunities to photograph the unusual animal and plant life we would encounter. Some collected the fragile rare orchids that grew high in the trees of the rain forest. Many soldiers collected the colorful butterflies and tropical fish that were indigenous to the jungles of Panama.

During weekends, there were a variety of recreational activities in which we could participate. The Army ran boat rental facilities on Gatun Lake for those soldiers and their families who enjoyed fishing for the plentiful peacock bass. There were historical ruins throughout Panama that could be explored. Day trips to some of Panama's more picturesque spots were scheduled for the servicemen and their families. We were truly "strangers in Paradise."

The plentiful beaches were magnificent and soldiers and their families could be found in droves on weekends, enjoying the two oceans that border the country. Some beaches had beautiful pearly white sand and boasted waves big enough on which to surf. Others were formed from ebony black volcanic sand that made walking painfully hot if one was not wearing sandals or other footwear.

Another activity many soldiers enjoyed at the beach was shelling. At least once a month the Pacific Ocean near Panama City would provide those of us interested in collecting seashells with a "minus tide." During these extremely low tides, shellers would walk out to places normally covered by water and gather live shelled animals to bring home for cleaning and oiling. This hobby was one that was enjoyed by many of the soldiers in the 601st Medical Company.

The families of the soldiers found life in Panama equally pleasant. The living quarters, for the most part, were superior to Army housing in other parts of the world. They were spacious and air-conditioned and the yards of the housing areas were full of tropical plants and were immaculately maintained. The neighborhood was very convenient to schools, shopping and public transportation. It was a comfortable and interesting place to live.

The commissary where we purchased our food was just down the hill from my quarters, making it easy for my wife, who did not drive, to shop. The edge of the jungle came up to my yard, allowing us to enjoy watching the animals that would come out of the wild in the evening to eat the fruit from the mango trees in our yard.

Kinkajous, small primates that looked like little teddy bears would use the tree to supply their dinner almost every night. Coatimundis, cousins to the American racoon, would brazenly approach children eating snacks and take the food from them if they refused to share their treats.

The youngsters in the neighborhood shared the mango tree's bounty with the animals of the jungle. Exotic tropical fruits were eaten with delight when soldier-parents brought them home from the jungle or when they were purchased at the local market. Other foods were equally plentiful and reasonably priced, especially for the braver soldiers who enjoyed shopping in Panama's central market. Steak could be purchased for about 38 cents a pound and fish was even cheaper and more abundant.

My three daughters particularly enjoyed the life they lived in Panama. After having spent a winter in Fort Dix, New Jersey before joining me in there, they appreciated the freedom of being able to go outside and play without having to bundle up. Another benefit of our four year tour in Panama was the fact that these three girls, who often experienced colds, earaches and sore throats when we lived in the United States, were virtually illness-free during the time we lived in Panama.

In November 1978, my daughters were ages 7, 4 and 3. On the 18th, my wife and I took them to the beach at Fort Kobe. It had a shark fence surrounding it, protecting swimmers from attacks by the fearsome fish that could frequently be seen swimming outside its perimeter. They and their friends were anticipating Thanksgiving which was only a few days away.

The military fathers and mothers of the children at the beach that Saturday were on the sand playing volleyball or sitting at picnic tables playing cards. Some were engaged in discussions about the "Panama Canal Zone give-away" that was in the news. Old Canal Zone residents were furious at President Jimmy Carter for threatening their way of life by proposing to turn the Canal Zone over to the Republic of Panama. It didn't matter much to the people I was socializing with, as soldiers and the families that accompanied them, this was just another duty station in a long string of assignments during an Army career.

While life in Panama was as good as it gets wherever American soldiers are stationed and even though the duty was more desirable than most places one could be posted to, it wasn't all fun and games. A soldier's mission in peace time is to prepare for war and that preparation is a lot of hard work. The 601st Medical Company was the field medical unit in the Canal Zone that was responsible for supporting virtually every 193rd Brigade field exercise that took place. If the 601st was not actually set up in the field, providing emergency medical treatment to the sick and injured, field ambulances from the company were there providing medical support during training exercises.

We were proud that of all the units in the command, for the most part, our's had a real-world mission. While the infantrymen of the 193rd played war games, our medics actually received hands-on real life experience caring for sick and injured soldiers. Occasionally, we would even go into a local town or village and support the Panama Defense Force when they provided medical treatment for isolated parts of the country that had no permanent medical facilities nearby.

The men and women of the 601st were satisfied with their lives, or at least as satisfied as soldiers can be. They stayed busy, actually did the jobs they were trained to do, and they did those jobs in a relatively pleasant environment. By 1978, all of them were volunteers and they were part of an Army that was becoming more soldier-oriented; an Army that cared about the comfort, health and welfare of its troops. It was the all-volunteer Army.

The good lives enjoyed by the American soldiers and their families in Panama were in sharp contrast to the lives of 914 other Americans who had journeyed to an alleged tropical paradise beginning in 1974. Jonestown, Guyana was approximately 1200 miles, as the crow flies, from Panama.

James Warren Jones, known as Reverend Jim Jones, was born in Lynn, Indiana on May 13, 1931. In the 1950's and '60's, in Indianapolis, Indiana, Jones gained a reputation as a charismatic preacher and clergyman. By 1963, he had his own religious congregation, the People's Temple Full Gospel Church. This incredibly dynamic orator led his interracial congregation with amazing faith healing, awesome visions and miraculous advice from extraterrestrials.

Jones moved his congregation from the city of Indianapolis to rural Ukiah, California in the early 1970's after having read that this region of the United States would be relatively safe from a nuclear attack. He was convinced that Indianapolis would be a major target of the Soviets when the inevitable nuclear war between the USA and USSR occurred and he convinced most of his simple parishioners to share his fear.

The move to Ukiah, where Jones formed the Peoples Temple, was soon followed by another move... this time to San Francisco. There he became a major social and political force, establishing a free health clinic and drug rehabilitation program. He even was appointed chairman of the San Francisco Housing Authority in 1976.

But soon, Jones was being attacked by former members of his church. He was accused of child abuse, misappropriation of the property of members, and even stealing the children of members.

Deborah Layton Blakey, a former Jones confidant, in an affidavit to the U.S. Justice Department taken on June 15, 1978, reported the reaction Jones had to these accusations. Blakey belonged to the People's Temple from August 1971 until May 13, 1978. She was the Financial Secretary of the church until she herself went to Guyana in December 1977.

"During the years I was a member of the People's Temple, I watched the organization depart with increasing frequency from its professional dedication for social change and participatory democracy. The Rev. Jim Jones gradually assumed a tyrannical hold over the lives of Temple members," wrote Blakey.

Jones regarded any disagreement with his dictates to be "treason." According to Blakey, he labeled any person who left the church a "traitor" and "fair game." He is said to have maintained that punishment for defection from the organization was death. Severe corporal punishment was frequently meted out to Temple members, giving the death threats a frightening air of reality.

Jones began to see himself as the victim of a conspiracy. His identification of the conspirators would frequently change, depending upon whatever vision of the world he had on a particular day. He told members of his congregation, that because he was their leader and he was a victim of conspiracy, they too were targets. He told black Temple members that if they did not follow him to Guyana, they would be put in concentration camps and killed.

According to Blakey, "White Temple members were instilled with the belief that their names appeared on a secret list of enemies of the state that was kept by the CIA and that they would be tracked down, tortured, imprisoned, and subsequently killed if they did not flee to Guyana."

By 1978, more than 1000 Americans, who believed strongly in Jim Jones, had left their homeland and journeyed to the sanctuary of Jonestown. One wonders how apparently intelligent adults could be taken in by such delusional thinking. But Jones was a master of deception. At Temple meetings he would talk non-stop for hours, his forceful charismatic voice carried over a loudspeaker system in the auditorium of the church building. His lieutenants would walk through the room waking up any member of the congregation who dared fall asleep during these marathon orations.

Jones claimed to be the reincarnation of Moses, Lenin and even Jesus Christ. He claimed he had divine powers and could heal the sick. He stated he had extra-sensory perception and could tell what people were thinking. He said he had powerful connections all over the world with the likes of the Mafia, the Soviet government and Idi Amin.

Blakey's affidavit states, "When I first joined the Temple, Rev. Jones seemed to make clear distinctions between fantasy and reality. I believed that most of the time when he said irrational things, he was aware that they were irrational, but they served as a tool of his leadership. His theory was that the end justifies the means. At other times, he appeared to be deluded by a paranoid vision of the world. He would not sleep for days at a time and talk compulsively about conspiracies against him. However, as time went on, he appeared to be genuinely irrational."

In Jonestown, 1200 miles from where I lived and worked in Panama, life for the transplanted Americans living there was very different than the one my family enjoyed. The vast majority of Jonestown residents worked in the fields from 7 AM to 6 PM six days a week and on Sunday from 7 AM until 2 PM. Blakey reported, "We were allowed one hour for lunch. Most of this hour was spent walking back to lunch and standing in line for our food. Taking any other breaks during the workday was severely frowned upon."

While food in Panama was plentiful and cheap, in Jonestown, meals were extremely basic and not very nutritious for most residents. Deborah Layton Blakey wrote in her affidavit, "The food was woefully inadequate. There was rice for breakfast, rice water soup for lunch, and rice and beans for dinner. On Sunday, we each received an egg and a cookie. Two or three times a week we had vegetables. Some very weak and elderly members received one egg per day."

Jim Jones enjoyed a much better diet than the members of his flock. Claiming he had problems with his blood sugar, he dined separately and ate meat regularly. Jones had his own refrigerator, well stocked with food.

The two women who lived with Jones, Maria Katsaris and Carolyn Layton and the two small boys who shared his quarters with him, Kimo Prokes and John Stoen, dined with the members. But Blakey reports these four were in much better physical shape than the other residents of Jonestown because they were allowed to eat the food from Jones' refrigerator.

"In February 1978, conditions had become so bad that half of Jonestown was ill with severe diarrhea and high fevers. I was seriously ill for two weeks. Like most of the other sick people, I was not given any nourishing foods to help recover. I was given water and a tea drink until I was well enough to return to the basic rice and beans diet," reported Blakey.

Blakey also stated in her affidavit that as financial secretary, she knew the Temple received over $65,000 in Social Security checks each month. "It made me angry to see that only a fraction of the income of the senior citizens in the care of the Temple was being used for their benefit," she wrote.

Jonestown had a very sophisticated state of the art loudspeaker system that Jones would use for up to six hours a day to broadcast his thoughts, threats and orders to every corner of the commune. When he was particularly agitated, he would rant and rave for far longer periods without stopping. He could be heard in the oppressively hot fields where the residents of Jonestown were toiled during the day. His loud voice would prevent his tired congregation from sleeping at night. Often at night, after work, there were meetings in the Pavilion that also lasted up to six hours. Jones seemed to be infatuated with his own voice and prophetic message.

Jones' paranoia caused his daily harangues and nightly meetings to be frightening affairs indeed. He was obsessed that his place in history had been irreparably ruined by the media. He felt their ridicule had caused him to lose an honored position in world affairs. He often complained that all was lost.

Deborah Layton Blakey reported, "There was constant talk of death. In the early days of the People's Temple, general rhetoric about dying for principles was sometimes heard. In Jonestown, the concept of mass suicide for socialism arose. Because our lives were so wretched anyway and because we were so afraid to contradict Rev. Jones, the concept was not challenged."

Mike Prokes, a dissatisfied follower of Jones and one of his enforcers, kept a diary. He was a survivor of the November 18, 1978 mass suicide/murder. Prokes notes were part of a collection of records that were sealed after the massacre at Jonestown. The contents of those records were opened in September 1988.

"I don't know how much longer I can take it," wrote Prokes. "I mean the witchcraft. I feel like I'm being programmed. I enjoy the violence when I do it, but sometimes like right now I feel sorry I did it."

"I think I'm going to end it all with my .38; I only wish I could see my brains blow out."

Ironically, Mike Prokes died a few months after the Jonestown Massacre. During a news conference, he pulled out his .38 and shot himself in the head.

Jones would declare a "White Night" or state of emergency at least once a week. This was ushered in by the blaring of loud sirens that would awaken the entire population of Jonestown. Jones' trusted lieutenants would move from cottage to cottage and make sure everyone was responding. All the residents would gather in the Pavilion for a mass meeting where they would be informed by Jones of some new crisis.

In her affidavit of June 15, 1978, Blakey wrote, "During one 'white night', we were informed that our situation had become hopeless and that the only course of action open to us was a mass suicide for the glory of socialism. We were told that we would be tortured by mercenaries if we were taken alive. Everyone, including the children, was told to line up. As we passed through the line, we were given a small glass of red liquid to drink. We were told that the liquid contained poison and that we would die within 45 minutes. We all did as we were told. When the time came when we should have dropped dead, Rev. Jones explained that the poison was not real and that we had just been through a loyalty test. He warned us that the time was not far off when it would become necessary for us to die by our own hands. Life at Jonestown was so miserable and the physical pain of exhaustion was so great that this event was not traumatic for me. I had become indifferent as to whether I lived or died."

"We would be told that the jungle was swarming with mercenaries and that death could be expected at any minute," reported Blakey.

These "White Nights" were bizarre rehearsals for the real moment when Jones would have his doctor and nurses dispense a potion of a cyanide combined with strong anticonvulsants, sedatives, hypnotics, tranquilizers and muscle relaxants mixed, not with grape Kool-Ade from the United States as popularly reported, but with Fla-Vor-Ade, a powdered drink mix manufactured in the United Kingdom.

Two very different groups of Americans were living in the tropics that November of 1978. One group living in a place called the best kept secret in the Army, another group of 914 living in another, better kept secret -- Jonestown, Guyana. One group enjoying the life in a tropical paradise, another group living a life that could only be characterized as Hell on earth.

Events that occurred on the 18th of November 1978, would inexorably connect members of these two groups with each other. As traumatic as what occurred in Jonestown was to its American expatriot residents, the trauma ended that evening for most of them. For those of us who were ordered from Panama to Guyana to become part of history, the trauma had yet to begin.

Two

Death in the Tropics

Congressman Leo J. Ryan was born in Lincoln Nebraska on May 5, 1925. Before being elected to Congress in 1973, Ryan had been a California state assemblyman for 10 years and was mayor of San Francisco in 1962.

Ryan's friends and enemies alike agreed he was brash and flamboyant. He was not afraid of a fight and spent much of his political life drawing attention to and trying to correct social abuses. After the Watts riots in 1965, Ryan, then a state legislator, went there and became a substitute teacher to investigate conditions in the black community. Because he wanted to be totally anonymous, he assumed a false identity. In 1970, he again went undercover with a different name and had himself sent to Folsom Prison to discover what life was really like there. In 1978, Ryan planned to go undercover as a Postal Service employee during the Christmas season to investigate complaints of bad working conditions. Ryan did not live to see Christmas in 1978.

By late 1977, Congressman Ryan had received dozens of unbelievable reports from constituents concerning the bizarre behavior of Rev. Jim Jones and strange goings-on in the People's Temple. Unfavorable magazine articles had been published about Jones and he was in a custody battle over a six-year-old boy he claimed was his "son." Most members of the church's congregation had moved to Jonestown, Guyana and by June of 1977, Jones himself had left the United States for the refuge he hoped would be provided for him in the isolated commune his followers had built in the jungles.

By the fall of 1978, defectors from the People's Temple and Jones' detractors were deluging Ryan with requests for action. Charges were being made that American citizens were being held against their will in Jonestown. Reports of terrible conditions abounded making it impossible for Congressman Ryan to ignore the desperate pleas of his constituents.

In November 1978, Ryan organized a trip to Guyana. His entourage included a small group of journalists, and a few concerned relatives of People's

Temple members who were living in Jonestown. These were the enemies most hated by Jones and his faithful followers; the dissident family members who had maligned him and his organization, the evil American press that had so willingly spread the lies of defectors, and the biggest evil of all, the United States government in the form of a cocky and self-important Congressman who seemed to enjoy making headlines.

At first, Jones steadfastly refused permission for the congressman's group to enter Jonestown. People's Temple members living there had written to Ryan, begging him not to visit because they felt he was intent on destroying their way of life. Ryan refused to back down or be dissuaded and Jones very reluctantly agreed to a short visit.

Congressman Ryan's party arrived in Jonestown late in the afternoon on November 17, 1978. During several meetings, they heard most residents praising the conditions in the commune and expressing their desire to remain there. However, on the second day of the visit, some newsmen found living quarters that were full of senior citizens laying in beds set up two or three inches from one another. The media representatives were denied access to other cottages they asked to visit, instead, being led to accommodations that had been prepared for their inspection prior to their arrival.

Notes were slipped to the congressman and members of his party by residents of Jonestown that desired to be taken home to the United States. Saturday, November 18, 1978 was not a good day for Jim Jones. His dreams were turning into nightmares. Sixteen residents of Jonestown had expressed a desire to leave Guyana. Overcrowded conditions were discovered by nosy newsmen.

As the visit neared the end, NBC news reporter Don Harris upset Jones as he asked incessant questions about guns, mind control, physical punishment and controlling of recalcitrant residents with drugs. It must have been obvious to Jones that some of the residents of Jonestown were talking about things he didn't want the world to know.

"Every major horror in history was commited in the name of an altruistic motive."

Ayn Rand

As the tension continued to mount and the 16 dissident residents were preparing to leave, one of Jones' most trusted lieutenants, Don Sly, grabbed Congressman Ryan from the back and held a knife to his neck. "Goddamn it motherfucker, you are not going to..." Sly started to shout as he was tackled by Mark Lane and Charles Garry, lawyers for the Temple, and others. Ryan was slightly wounded during the incident as was Sly.

Despite the altercation, Ryan told Jones that his report would be a positive one. He said he had not seen any coercion being used to keep people in Jonestown. As the Ryan party left for the airstrip, a black pall hung over Jonestown. One woman could be heard screaming because her husband and children were among the 16 who were leaving.

Within an hour or so after the Ryan party left Jonestown for the airstrip at Port Kaitumba, Jones Lieutenant Larry Layton arrived back at Jonestown, after his unsuccessful attempt to stop the defections by trying to kill all members of the Ryan group along with the defectors. He approached Jones who was still sitting on his wooden throne in the pavilion and carried on a short, whispered conversation with him.

Layton had left for Port Kaitumba with six other armed men shortly before the Ryan party left Jonestown. At the air strip, the Jones loyalists opened fire on the Ryan group, killing Ryan, Patty Park, a member of Jones' congregation since it was founded in Indiana, Don Harris and two other newsmen and wounding several others in the group. One can only speculate on what Layton said to his leader, but by Jones' reaction, it was obvious the news was not good.

Jones immediately called for a "White Night." He ordered the commune's physician, Larry Schact, and his nurses to prepare the deadly brew that would soon be used to kill most of the residents of Jonestown. Then, Jones turned on his tape recorder and methodically called his congregation to assemble together for the last time.

The chilling audio tape Jones made that November 18 in 1978 as the final ritual of this religious group was being enacted is shocking in its content; but it gives us an insight into why 913 Americans would, for the most part, willingly take their lives. A more complete transcript is found in the Appendix.

Jones: I've tried my best to give you a good life. In spite of all I've tried, a handful of people, with their lies, have made our life impossible. If we can't live in peace the let's die in peace. [Applause]... We have been so terribly betrayed. We have been so terribly betrayed. [Music and singing] What's going to happen here in a matter of a few minutes is that one of the people on that plane is going to shoot the pilot - I know that. I didn't plan it, but I know it is going to happen. They're going to shoot that pilot and down comes the plane into the jungle. And we better not have any of our children left when it's over. Because they'll parachute in here on us... So my opinion is that you be kind to children, and be kind to seniors, and take the potion like they used to take in ancient Greece, and step over quietly, because we are not committing suicide - it's a revolutionary act... We can't go back... Anybody. Anyone that has any dissenting opinion, please speak. Yes. You can have an opportunity, but if the children are left, we're going to have them butchered...

Woman: Well, I don't see it like that. I mean, I feel like that as long as there's life there's hope. That's my faith.

Jones: Well, someday everybody dies. Some place that hope runs out; because everybody dies. I haven't seen anybody yet didn't die. And I like to choose my own kind of a death for a change. I'm tired of being tormented to hell, that's what I'm tired of. Tired of it [Applause].

Crowd: That's right. That's right!

Jones: What those people gone and done, and what they get through will make our lives worse than hell... But to me, death is not a fearful thing. It's living that's cursed... Not worth living like this.

Woman: I said I'm not ready to die.

Jones: I don't think you are. I don't think you are...

Woman: I look at all the babies and I think they deserve to live...

Jones: But don't they deserve much more they deserve peace. The best testimony we can give is to leave this goddamn world. [Applause]... Lay down your burden. I'm gonna lay down my burden. Down by the riverside. Shall we lay them down here by the side of Guyana? No man didn't take our lives. Right now. They haven't taken them. But when they start parachuting out of the air, they'll seek some of our innocent babies. I'm not -- I don't want... They've got to shoot me to get through to some of the people. I'm not telling them take your child. Can you let them take your child?

Voices: No. No. No.

Jones: I want to see...

[Many voices shouting and talking at once]

Jones: Please. Please. Please. Please. Please. Please.

Man: I'm ready to go. If you tell us we have to give our lives now, we're ready. [Applause] All the rest of the brothers and sisters are with me.

Second Man: It's over sister... We've made a beautiful day. [Applause]

The tape continues. Babies can be heard wailing, adult voices are shouting nervously and Jones insists suicide must happen and urges his people to complete the act:

Jones: Please get some medication. Simple. It's simple. There's's no convulsions with it... Just, please, get it. Before it's too late. The G.D.F. [Guyana Defense Force] will be here, I tell you. Get movin', get movin', get movin'.

[Voices]

Jones: Don't be afraid to die. You'll see people land out here. They'll torture our people...

Second Woman: There's nothing to worry about. Everybody keep calm and try to keep your children calm... They're not crying from pain; it's just a little bitter tasting...

Third Woman: This is nothing to cry about. This is

something we could all rejoice about. [Applause]

Jones: Let's make our peace. And those had a right to go, and they had a right to -- how many are dead? Aw,, God, Almighty God. Huh? Patty Park is dead?

[Voices]

Jones: I don't know how in the world they're ever going to write about us. It's just too late. It's too late. The congressman's dead. The... Many of our... are dead. They're all laying out there dead... Please can we hasten? Can we hasten with our medication? You don't know what you've done. I tried. [Applause and music]

Woman: Do... have to know when the people that are standing there in the aisles. Go stand in the radio room yard... OK, there's nothing to worry about...

Third Man: So much to do before I came here. So let me tell you about it. It may make a lot of you feel more comfortable. Sit down and be quiet please. One of the things I used to do -- I used to be a therapist. And the kind of therapy that I did had to do with reincarnation in past life situations. And every time anybody had an experience of going into a past life, I was fortunate enough through Father [Jones] to be able to let them experience it all the way through their death, so to speak. And everybody was so happy when they made that step to the other side.

Fourth Woman: I just want to say something for everyone that I see standing around, or crying. This is nothing to cry about. This is something we all could rejoice about. We could be happy about this. I was just thinking about Jim Jones. He has suffered and suffered and suffered. We have the honor guard and we don't even have the chance to... here... one more chance. That's few that's gone. There's' many more here... That's not all of us. That's not all, yet. That's just a few that have died. I'm looking at so many people crying. I wish you would not cry. [Applause] I've been here one year and nine months. And I never felt better in my life. Not in San Francisco. But until I came to Jonestown. I had a... life. I had a beautiful life. We should be happy. At least I am. [applause]

Fourth Woman: Good to be alive today. I just like to thank Dad [Jones] 'cause he was the only one that stood up for me when I needed him. And thank you, Dad.

Fifth Woman: I'm glad that you're my brothers and sisters. I'm glad to be here.

[Voices]

Jones: Please. For God's sake, let's get on with it. We've lived - we've lived as no other people lived and loved.

We've had as much of this world as your gonna get. Let's just be done with it. Let's be done with the agony of it.

[Applause]

[Voices]

Jones: -- wants to go with their child has a right to go with their child. I think it's humane. I want to go - I want to see you go though. They can take me and do what they want -

whatever they want to do. I want to see you go. I don't want to see you go through this hell no more. No more. No more... We're trying. If everybody - relax. The best thing you can do is relax and you won't have no problem with this thing. If you just relax.

By now, there were apparently a large number of babies and children who had already been murdered by their own mothers. A fifth man mentions this fact next:

Fifth Man: - a great deal because it's Jim Jones. And the way the children are laying there now. I'd rather see them lay like that than to see them die like the Jews did, which was pitiful anyhow. And I just like to thank Dad, who gave them this life, and also death. And I appreciate the fact the way our children are going. Because, like Dad said, when they came in. What they're gonna do to our children - they're gonna massacre our children. And also the ones they take capture [sic], they're gonna just let them grow up and be dummies, just like they want them to be. And not grow up to be a person like the one and only Jim Jones. So I'd like to thank Dad for the opportunity for letting Jonestown be not what it could be, but what Jonestown is.

Thank you Dad. [Applause]

Sixth Man: It is not to be feared. It is not to be feared. It is a friend. It's a friend. Sitting there show your love for one another. Take your time -

Jones: Let's get gone. Let's get gone. Let's get gone. We had nothing we could do. We can't separate ourselves from our own people. For twenty years lying in some old rotten nursing home. Taking us through all these anguish years... I don't know who fired the shot. I don't know who killed the congressman. But as far as I'm concerned, I killed him. You understand what I am saying.

Second Woman: Right. Right.

[Music and children crying]

Jones: I, with respect, die with the beginning of dignity. Lay down your life with dignity. Don't lay down with tears and agony. It's nothing to death. It's like Mac said, it's stepping over to another plane. Don't be this way. Stop this hysterics. This is not the way for people who are

Socialists or Communists to die. No way for us to die. We must die with some dignity... we have no choice. Now we have some choice. Do you think they're gonna allow this to be done? And allow us to get by with this? You must be insane - children, it's just something to put you to rest. Oh God!

Apparently, at this point, some of the women who had killed their own offspring were wailing uncontrollably. Jones seems to become nervous and agitated, possibly fearing that their spontaneous display of agonizing remorse would become contagious and infect those mothers who had not yet decided to force the poisonous drink down the throats of their own children.

[Children crying / women wailing]

Jones: Mother, mother, mother, mother, mother, please. Mother, please, please, please, please, please. Don't do this. Lay down your life with your child. But don't do this... Free at Last!. Keep -keep your emotions down. Keep your emotions down. Children, it will not hurt. If you'd be - if you'd be quiet.

[Music, children crying]

Jones: ...I don't care how many screams you hear. I don't care how many anguished cries. Death is a million times preferable to spend(ing) more days in this life. If you knew what was ahead of you - if you knew what was ahead of you, you'd be glad to be stepping over tonight... Let's be digni - let's be dignified. If you quit telling them they're dying - if you would also stop some of this nonsense - adults, adults, I call upon you to stop this nonsense. I call on you to quit exciting your children, when all they're doing is going to a quiet rest. I call on you to stop this now, if you have any respect at all. Are we black, proud, Socialist - or what are we? Now stop this nonsense. Don't carry on like this anymore. You are exciting your children... All over and it's good. No - no sorrow that it's all over. I'm glad it's over. Hurry, Hurry my children. Hurry. All I - the hands of the enemy. Hurry my children. Hurry. There are seniors out there that I'm concerned about. Hurry. I don't want any of my seniors to this mess. Only quickly, quickly,

quickly, quickly, quickly. Let's just - Good knowing you... No more pain, Al. No more pain, I said, Al. No more pain... All they do is take a drink. They take it to go to sleep. That's what death is, sleep - I'm tired of it all... Take our life from us. We laid it down. We got tired. We didn't commit suicide, we committed an act of revolutionary suicide protesting the conditions of an inhumane world.

[Organ music]

The children were the first to be fed the deadly brew concocted by physician Larry Schact and his team of loyal nurses. Then the mothers who took the young lives of their very own sons and daughters joined them in death. Next it was the many senior citizens who Jones had convinced to flee to Guyana that were given their final drink on earth. The rest of the adults soon followed the children, mothers and seniors to complete this horrific ritualistic act of mass murder/suicide.

While Congressman Ryan and his party of concerned family members, news reporters and defectors were riding in a truck toward mayhem and death at the small air strip of Port Kaitumba, some five miles north of Jonestown, my family and I were driving the five miles or so from Kobe Beach to the Corazal Army Housing area.

As the maniacal Rev. Jim Jones was exhorting his flock to commit the final revolutionary act of mass suicide, my wife was feeding my three daughters their supper and I was on my way to pick up the babysitter who would safeguard and protect them while we went to the casino at the Granada Hotel for our bimonthly gambling spree.

As mothers in Jonestown were dosing their children with a deadly potion and carefully laying them down on the ground to die, in Panama, the mother of my children was lovingly bathing them, putting on their pajamas and tucking them into their beds. I had no idea that by the next morning, I would be forever connected to this group of now deceased Americans 1200 miles away in Guyana and that our activities of November 18 had contrasted so closely with theirs.

We went to the casino that Saturday night just as we had twice monthly since my family had joined me in Panama. We conducted our regular recreational ritual at the same time the residents of Jonestown were practicing a ritual they had rehearsed for well over a year. They were conducting their's for the final time.

Odell Rhodes, one of the very few survivors of the Jonestown Massacre graphically described to newsmen the horror he witnessed in Jonestown as Rev. Jim Jones called his congregation to their final "White Night."

"They started with the babies," Rhodes told journalist Charles Krause. He told him most of the adults who drank the cyanide-laced Fla-Vor-Ade did so willingly.

Larry Schact, Jonestown's doctor and his nurses mixed the deadly potion. Rhodes told Krause that many of the mothers would poison their own children before taking the cyanide drink themselves. Several who tried to escape the mass suicide ritual were herded back to the center of the community where the poisonous brew was forced upon them. This was before the mass killings and suicides began.

Rhodes said then, "It just got all out of order. Babies were screaming, children were screaming and there was mass confusion." He said it took about five minutes for the deadly liquid to kill its victims.

Rhodes said that young and old, black and white, grouped themselves near family members, often with their arms around one another, waiting for the cyanide to take effect.

Despite the anticonvulsants, muscle relaxants, sedatives and other drugs that were mixed with the cyanide, Rhodes reported those who partook of the poison would go into convulsions. Their eyes would roll up, they would gasp for breath and then they would be dead.

Apparently Dr. Schact was not as knowledgeable of the effects of the psychotropic drugs he added to his evil brew as he was the poison he used to kill the residents of Jonestown. While the cyanide took less than five minutes to cause those who ingested it to go into horrible convulsions and die, the tranquilizers and sedatives added to the potion to counteract that effect took around fifteen minutes to begin working.

All the while, during the time mothers were killing their babies and children with the cyanide mixture, Jones urged them on over the commune's loudspeaker system. When the children were all dead or near death, he told the able-bodied adults to tend to the seniors. When the oldest members of the congregation had finished taking this bizarre communion drink, it was time for the rest of the residents to die.

Rhodes watched this final White Night in horror. He was desperate to escape, but knew if he panicked and fled, the poison would be forced down his throat as it was the others. But when Dr. Larry Schact said he needed a stethoscope, Rhodes saw his opportunity to get away from the center of the mass suicide activity and he volunteered to accompany a nurse to the infirmary, about 300 feet away and bring a stethoscope back to the doctor.

Rhodes told Krause that armed guards let him through with the nurse and he hid under a building while she went into the doctor's office to fetch the stethoscope. By 7 PM, all sound had ceased in Jonestown. The entire killing of nearly 1000 people had occurred in a period of less than two-and-one-half hours. As the sun began to set, an eerie silence fell upon the commune. The voice of Rev. Jim Jones, usually heard for at least six hours a day over the loud speaker system, was never to be heard again, except in tapes Jones himself recorded of the massacre that he set into motion that November 18. Blessed silence had replaced the sounds of crying children and wailing mothers. The barking of the many dogs that lived among the residents was absent as well, for the dogs, along with the humans had been put to death.

Rhodes, slowly left the safety and sanctuary he had enjoyed under the building and ventured carefully out into the compound. Everywhere he looked there was death. Bodies, mostly laying in groups, could be seen in every direction.

Rhodes wearily walked from Jonestown to Port Kaitumba where he alerted Guyanese authorities to the tragedy that had befell his community and his friends a few hours before. The next morning, a contingent of Guyanese Defense Force troops was dispatched to Jonestown to verify the bizarre story Odell told authorities.

News of the events that occurred in Jonestown on the afternoon and evening of November 18 took a very short time to filter out to the rest of the world. When it did, the United States government reacted with unprecedented speed. On Sunday November 19, military troops in Fort Bragg, North Carolina, Fort Lee, Virginia, Dover Air Force Base, Delaware, Charleston Air Force Base, South Carolina and in the Panama Canal Zone were put on alert for movement to Guyana. They had no idea what they were getting us into and we were given little direction.

Speculation was rampant and unrestrained. Rumors of hostile cult members hiding in the jungle waiting to ambush us abound. Why were these Americans living in Guyana and why did they choose to try to take their lives? Was this a mysterious crisis being perpetrated by the Russians who were known to have close relations with Guyana? Were the Cubans involved?

The rumor mill ground out every possible scenario. All too soon we were to witness the aftermath of what grotesque carnage had been wrought against 913 innocent souls by the twisted but persuasive mind of one "Reverend" James Warren Jones.

> "No man is an Island, entire of itself; every man is a piece of the Continent, a part of the main; if a clod be washed away by the sea, Europe is the less, as well as if a promontory were, as well as if a manor of thy friends or of thine own were; any man's death diminishes me, because I am involved in Mankind; and therefore never send to know for who the bell tolls; it tolls for thee."
>
> **John Donne**
> **Meditation XVII**

Three

"We aren't prepared for this"

I'm not sure when the 193rd Infantry Brigade Emergency operation Center received the first notification that something terrible had happened to several hundred American living in the jungles of Guyana, but I was informed by First Sergeant Phil Arthur at about 9 AM Sunday November 19. A phone call alerted me that my immediate presence was required in the company. I was the Chief Wardmaster of the Clearing Platoon and it wasn't unusual for a meeting to be called on the weekend, particularly if the skills and assets of the medical company were needed to respond to some natural disaster. I wasn't sure what calamity caused this meeting to be called, but I was quite certain it wasn't an earthquake or hurricane as none had been reported on the news. Usually Top would tell me the reason for such a weekend meeting. This time he did not.

I quickly changed from the shorts and T-shirt that was my standard weekend uniform into tropical fatigues. The battle dress uniform that is currently worn by soldiers was not yet in the inventory. After kissing my kids and wife goodbye I explained to them I'd return home as soon as possible. Being veteran Army "brats" and a dutiful Army wife, the family took my departure in stride as it had dozens of times in the past.

Arriving at the 601st Medical Company, I noticed the brigade surgeon's and company commander's cars were in the parking lot. It was most unusual for the Brigade Surgeon to be present at an initial predeployment briefing. It was a somber scene in the commander's office. The faces that greeted me were not the ordinarily jovial ones normally exhibited by these professionals. Even when a soldier's weekend is interrupted by some emergency or disaster, he usually maintains his sense of humor. Obviously some major calamity was brewing!

"What's up sirs?," I said, addressing my commander who was Captain Robert Snow and the Brigade Surgeon who was Major Vincent Buenos.

Buenos was a seasoned Army doctor and an excellent Brigade Surgeon. He knew all of the standard policies, procedures, and protocols and he operated by them. Once, when a tracked vehicle fell from a bridge, gruesomely killing one of the occupants, I watched him adroitly treat one of the soldiers who saw his buddy die instantly before his eyes.

The young soldier luckily had no physical injuries but he was a psychological mess. He was brought into our clearing station on a litter. He had soiled himself and was shaking so badly he could not hold a cigarette. The soldier could not or would not talk. After assessing the casualty's physical condition, Major Buenos told me to admit him to the ward, clean him up and get him a bed.

"Don't you want to send him to Gorgas [Army Hospital] for psychiatric evaluation?" I asked the Brigade Surgeon.

"What's the philosophy behind treating a psychiatric casualty in combat, Brailey?" he replied.

"Treat him as close as you can to the front line and then get him back to duty as soon as you can," I correctly responded. In combat, psychiatric casualties recover better if they are allowed to return to their unit and comrades as quickly as possible.

"But this isn't combat, Doc, this is a field exercise," I said, "Do you think the philosophy applies here?"

"Of course it does," said Buenos. "We train like we fight. In a few hours that soldier will be able to hold his own cigarette, will be talking to the other patients and will eat dinner. By tomorrow morning I expect I'll send him back to duty."

That afternoon I wandered back to the ward tent to check on the soldier who witnessed the horrible death of his friend. He was sitting on the edge of his cot, smoking a cigarette. He was able to hold it by himself, but he wasn't very talkative. A few hours later, the soldier was eating his dinner and telling his fellow bunkmates about the terribly traumatic accident. By the next morning he was anxious to get back to his unit and perform his duties.

I told Major Buenos that I was impressed by the recovery of the initially autistic soldier. He took it in stride and asked if there were lessons to be learned about human behavior as a result of this tragic accident. His point was well taken. I learned a lot about medicine from Major Vincent Buenos, but on this Sunday, November 19, 1978, even he didn't know what we should do and his bewilderment was disconcerting.

Buenos looked at the three men in the room with him. Phil Arthur was a First Sergeant. Eight years before, he was my supervisor in Vietnam, and was one of the finest noncommissioned officers I ever served with. We had been back together only a few short months. Captain Robert Snow was the company commander of the 601st Medical Company. He was a no-nonsense Medical Service Corps officer, very short in stature, who seemed to have an inferiority complex about his height, but he was one of the most competent Medical Service Corps officers I ever served under.

I was the third person Buenos was looking at. As a Specialist 6th Class, I was the lowest ranking man in the room. However, I was a Vietnam veteran, who did two tours in 'Nam and was one of only a handful of NCO's in the company with combat experience. Having served in the 601st for two years and four months as of November 1978, I was in charge of the inpatient and Admissions &

Disposition sections of the clearing platoon which made up the hospital wards and emergency room.

Buenos told us what little he knew, which wasn't much. Basically he said, "A bunch of Americans living in Guyana have attempted mass suicide by taking poison... maybe 400 to 500 people, men women and children. We don't know what they took. We don't know how many are still alive. We are going to be part of a task force to go there and assess the situation, assist the survivors and bring the remains of the dead out of Guyana."

I looked Buenos in the eye and said, "Sir, we aren't prepared for this." Nothing in our combined experience could prepare us for the shocking hell of Jonestown.

A Medical Clearing Company is made up of around 112 soldiers. It has a bed capacity of 100 patients. While it has the capabilities of most hospitals; an emergency room (called Admissions & Disposition), wards, a laboratory, x-ray department and operating room, it is designed to function under combat conditions. Traumatic injuries, not mass poisonings, are the types of casualties this medical unit is set up to receive.

We had very little information about what had happened in Guyana and to whom it had happened. All we knew is that perhaps some 500 Americans had attempted suicide by taking an unknown poison. The universal antidote for poisoning is activated charcoal mixed in water. We had plenty of water, but were not sure how we could locate enough activated charcoal to treat that number of poisoning cases. Even if we could locate the proper antidotes in an adequate amount, what condition would any survivors be in once we arrived at their remote jungle location some 1200 miles away?

We were tasked with an unusual and unique mission and we had to do the best we could with limited resources to accomplish the grisly assignment. Major Buenos was going to put the antidote kit together that would be used to treat any survivors. Selecting a team to provide that treatment and to care for any injuries or casualties that might occur incidental to the mission became my responsibility.

This was done with considerable care. Ben Samuels, another Specialist Six practical nurse like myself, would be one of our team members. Ben was a quiet but very competent soldier-medic who was fairly new to the 601st.

Rick Fields, a Specialist Fourth Class "mini-charlie" would be another member. A mini-charlie was a new breed of medic; one who had only completed half the practical nurse course before being assigned to a unit. The Army was not happy that the "full-charlies" were leaving the Army in droves for better paying jobs in the civilian sector. The inadequate answer to this problem was to have mini-charlies who were not as well trained as the full-charlies but were slotted in units as if they had completed the course. If they reenlisted, the mini-charlies were allowed to go to an advanced school and become full-charlies. It was an ill-fated experiment in retention that thankfully ended soon after it began.

Fields was a very resourceful soldier. He was able to drive any vehicle the Army had and wasn't afraid of work. Better yet, of all the younger soldiers, he was one of the more well- liked by the higher ranking NCOs and he fit in well with the composition of our team.

Mark Sanders was a Specialist Four as well. He was a 91A Combat medic. As big and strong as an ox, Sanders could be counted on to get the job done, no matter how great the hardship. He reacted well in bad situations and the more difficult things were the harder the young soldier worked to complete the mission.

It was decided that Captain Snow and Major Buenos would also be members of the group. The last two soldiers to make up the eight-man team were Specialists Fourth Class Juan Rivera and Clint Yoakum. They were medical records specialists who would be needed if a large number of survivors were to be treated by our contingent. Unfortunately, when we arrived in Georgetown, Guyana, we learned there were no survivors of the Jonestown Massacre. Rivera and Yoakum remained in Georgetown as part of the labor force that unloaded the remains of 914 American citizens from the helicopters that had lifted them out of the jungle death camp presided over by Jim Jones.

We quickly assembled the equipment and supplies we would be taking to Guyana, checking each item to make sure drugs were not outdated and all equipment was workable. This was all placed on pallets and transported by truck to Howard Air Force Base. After that task was completed, the team members went to their respective quarters to pack their personal clothing and equipment and to say goodbye to their families.

We didn't know how long we would be gone, but it was a safe bet we would not be spending Thanksgiving in Panama with our loved ones. Although military people are notorious for spending the holidays away from their families due to official duties, this would be the first major holiday away from my wife and three daughters.

We had been married a little over seven years at the time. My oldest daughter, Suzanne, was born in Vietnam during my second tour of duty there. The other two girls, Jennifer and Deborah were born at Fort Dix New Jersey, exactly 364 days apart, on February 21, 1974 and February 20, 1975. Suzy's birthday is February 18 so group birthdays were celebrated on Valentine's Day until the girls became individual enough to want their own parties.

The food for our family Thanksgiving feast was already in the refrigerator and freezer. The first sergeant and his wife said they would make sure our families would be safe and sound during our absence, as was the unit tradition when soldiers had to be away.

After storing the essentials in my duffle bag and saying goodbye to my family, I went straight to the company. From there we were transported to Howard Air

Force Base and loaded on C-130s for five hour flights to Georgetown, Guyana.

The Air Force C-130 is a flying workhorse. Passengers sit in seats made of nylon netting and cargo is stowed in the middle of the aircraft. Many people have difficulty sleeping on a commercial airliner, but give me the hammock-like seat of a C-130, let me listen to the loud drone of its engines for a few minutes and its off to dreamland. The engines are quite loud, making conversation difficult. Since none of us knew what we were getting ourselves into and no one could talk over the sounds of the engines and be easily understood, most of the passengers on our flight rested or read during the entire trip.

It was a star-filled night when we left Panama's air space. The fact that the mission we were embarking on was undoubtedly one of the most unusual in the annals of military history added to the uneasiness one feels when it is dark and the senses are handicapped. Nothing could be seen outside the aircraft except blackness and the noise of the engines made communications next to impossible. I guess this was one of the few times in my Army career when I truly felt like a mushroom: kept in the dark and fed bullshit. Only this time, we didn't even have the B. S.

The sun was just a thin red line on the eastern horizon when we arrived at Timerhi Airport near Georgetown Guyana. Even though we were tropical soldiers stationed in Panama, the stifling humid heat of that South American country was somewhat overwhelming as the Air Force crew opened the huge back hatch on the aircraft. Unlike Panama, the rainy season was in full swing in Guyana and the humidity was overwhelming.

Upon disembarking from the Hercules C-130, we were assembled in what was obviously an unused terminal. One look across the expanse of runways, about half a mile away explained why: a gleaming new terminal could be seen on the other side. I do not know if we were purposely segregated from the civilian population of Georgetown, but in a briefing given by Colonel William Gordon, our task force commander, we were told that any place but where we now were was off limits. We were especially forbidden to go anywhere near the civilian terminal across the tarmac and were not allowed to speak with any one not associated with the operation.

This is not unusual for many missions soldiers go on and once we realized the international and social implications of what occurred in Jonestown, just two days before, these rules made perfect sense for this situation. Interestingly and unbeknownst to us, hundreds of journalists were located at the new terminal, some had long range lenses on their cameras and had them aimed in our direction most of the time. A pulp tabloid magazine quickly drafted a "special edition" about the Jonestown Tragedy. It was quickly slapped together and published within days after it occurred. Three soldiers from our team adorned its cover. The very grainy photo had obviously been shot with an extremely long range telephoto lens.

We arrived in Georgetown early on the morning of November 20. The victims of the Jonestown Massacre had been laying where they fell or placed themselves after ingesting their poisonous potion during the evening on November 18. The tropical heat is not kind to formerly living tissue and after this length of time in the sun and stifling heat, Jonestown was most assuredly a very unpleasant place to be. This was one of the subjects we discussed as we waited to see what our next move was.

Colonel William Gordon was the forward commander of this Joint Task Force. Although I didn't know it at the time, his temporary command consisted of personnel from every branch of service. There were Graves Registration soldiers from a unit stationed in Fort Lee, Virginia. A clearing platoon, much like the 601st that I was assigned to was coming in from Fort Bragg, North Carolina as well. It was to be set up here at Timerhi Airport. Special Forces soldiers from Fort Gulick, Panama had accompanied us on our aircraft as did some soldiers whose specialty was aviation fuel. Airmen from Charleston Air Force Base also made up part of the task force. And Colonel Gordon was in charge of it all.

Gordon was an old soldier in 1978. His demeanor was always professional, but he was very easy to talk with and really enjoyed leading men. Unquestionably, he was a good leader too. Gordon was jovial when he wanted to be and stern when he needed to be. When he talked, his soldiers listened and responded appropriately. Mrs. Gordon was a member of the Ancon Theater Guild back in Panama and so was I. Colonel Gordon and I knew each other socially, but this was the first opportunity I had to be in his direct chain of command.

I assume Colonel Gordon was privy to all of the intelligence being provided the US Government about Jonestown and what happened there. Maybe Major Buenos was also briefed well and knew almost as much as Gordon did. It is probable even Captain Snow was in the loop, at least to some degree. I do know that none of the other enlisted men, nor myself, received one briefing about what happened in Jonestown or what it was like there at the moment we were waiting to go in there.

After lounging around the old airport terminal for around two hours, we learned that my team would be leaving soon. A Guyanese Airliner that normally holds around 30 passengers had been configured for cargo. That means all of its seats had been removed. None of the helicopters that were flown in from Panama were ready to fly as of yet. The big Air Force H-53 "Jolly Green Giant" choppers being shuttled down to Guyana from the United States had not arrived.

Anyone who served in Vietnam holds fond memories of the Jolly Green Giants. Their sole mission was to rescue downed aircraft crews and GIs on clandestine ground operations behind enemy lines. The Air Force had deployed in two squadrons to Indochina. One was stationed at Da Nang, South Vietnam and the other at NKP, Thailand. Together they made over 2,600 "combat saves." While rescuing the fortunate 2,600, the two gallant squadrons sustained the loss of 65 of their own crew members.

We had to rely on the Guyanese for air transport. The small yellow and white Guyanese Airways aircraft taxied over to where our pallets of material sat on the hot black tarmac. I noticed it was a 747, but it bore no resemblance to the huge aircraft the Boeing Aircraft Corporation produced for commercial passenger service. After loading all of our equipment into the aircraft we were told to get in ourselves and find a floor space anywhere we could. This was the first time I had ever ridden an airplane where there was no seat belt to fasten nor even a seat in which to buckle up.

We had put our cargo all along the floor of the aircraft and it appeared to be fairly evenly distributed. Neither the Guyanese pilot nor the co-pilot had checked the weight of our equipment. Nor was there any inquiry as to the combined weight of the cargo or the twelve men on board. The aircraft seemed to take forever to get airborne and I seriously worried that perhaps it was considerably overloaded. Silence prevailed; but, we all shared the same concerns.

I did find out that we were en route to Matthews Ridge, a small bauxite mining town approximately 20 miles southwest of Jonestown. The accessible bauxite had long been extracted from the mines around Matthews Ridge so this previously bustling frontier town was in severe decline. It did have an airstrip about three miles away from the quaint little town. That was to become our base camp until the end of the mission; that being returning the remains of the dead Americans back to the United States.

At this time, it was believed there were some 400 dead. A few survivors were said to have managed to escape the mass suicide ritual by running into the jungle and finding their way to either Port Kaitumba or Matthews Ridge by following an old rail line.

We arrived at the airstrip just before noon on November 20, 1978. After the mighty Guyanese Airways 747 landed, it taxied to the end of the runway, near the Guyana Defense Force outpost. We unloaded our equipment and carried it up a small hill to a flat area, ideal for pitching our tent. After exchanging introductions and pleasantries with some of the local Guyana Defense Force troops, we decided to eat a C-ration lunch since we had not had a meal since the night before. This break gave us the opportunity to meet some of the local citizens of Matthews Ridge.

> "The beauty of religious mania is that it has the power to explain everything. Once God (or Satan) is accepted as the first cause of everything which happens in the mortal world, nothing is left to chance... logic can be happily tossed out the window."
>
> Stephen King

Four

John Wayne Bars and Other Treats

As we were unloading our equipment and toting it up the hill about 50 yards away from the edge of the tarmac, the children and teenagers of Matthews Ridge began to appear. Within an hour, we had quite a large group of young onlookers. The ethnic breakdown of Guyana is mainly blacks, Indians from India and Amerindians who were indigenous to the country.

The group of locals that was watching us were made up of mostly blacks with a few Amerindians. Two delightful almond-colored young girls drew closer to me as I sat on a rock and began opening my c-ration meal. C-rations were not the best tasting cuisine ever created, but when you were hungry, they were filling and loaded with carbohydrates and calories for the energy soldiers require. My particular meal contained beans and franks, canned peaches, peanut butter, and a small tin that contained crackers and two candy discs euphemistically called "John Wayne" Bars, a phrase coined during the Vietnam Era.

As I opened my main course with the P-38 tool every experienced field soldier wears around his neck, the two curious teenage girls came and sat on either side of me. Although very hungry myself, out of courtesy, it seemed appropriate to share some of my meal with them. The meal packet contained two John Wayne Bars so I handed one to each of these young beauties.

The girl on my right, her name was Pauline, studied the aluminum foil wrapping encasing the chocolate candy that had bits of almond and crunchy nougat in it. "What is this?" Pauline inquired. "Why it's candy," was my reply. "What type of candy?" she asked, still studying the wrapper.

"It's a chocolate bar," I answered. Almost before I finished my short four word reply, Pauline eagerly peeled the foil wrapper from her John Wayne Bar and stuffed the entire disc into her mouth, ravishing it in a single bite. Her little friend did likewise.

"What's the matter with you?" I asked as she greedily licked the tiny slivers of chocolate from around her lips.

"I've never eaten chocolate before," came Pauline's simple explanation in a crisp British accent that all of the Americans found enchanting when emitted from the mouths of these simple native people.

"Oh come on!" was my suspicious response. "Doesn't your mother allow you to eat candy?"

"We don't have chocolate in this country," Pauline said. That simple explanation sounded unbelievable, but a Guyanese Defense Force soldier who was standing nearby talking to Fields confirmed her statement.

"It's a luxury," he said. "Guyana has a problem with its balance of trade so we don't import luxuries if we can help it."

Word quickly spread around Matthews Ridge that the American soldiers staying at the airfield had chocolate candy and soon every female teenager in the region was visiting us, trying to be lucky enough to receive a John Wayne Bar or one of the other two less desirable chocolate treats, chocolate fudge and chocolate and coconut, found in the c-ration meals. It nearly got out of hand. The girls were becoming bolder and bolder in their attempts to befriend an American soldier who would be willing to give them chocolate. One of my soldiers was a handsome and very outgoing young black American had no trouble finding some local Guyanese women to flirt with. Another young man had his share of women working on him hard and often in the hopes he would favor them with a treat. GIs that served in World War II, Korea and Vietnam reported similar pleasant incidents that happened during their tours of duty.

Captain Snow and Major Buenos stayed with us during the first day we set up at Matthew's Ridge, but by that night, both returned to Georgetown, where the command structure of the task force was located. They flew into Jonestown in a Guyana Defense Force helicopter for a tour of Jonestown immediately after we arrived.

With the two officers gone, it was up to me to make sure order was maintained. Ben Samuels was no problem; like me, he was an old married man. But Fields and Sanders were another story altogether. They were in their early 20s and had yet to attain complete control over their hormones. But they were well-disciplined and knew they would endure the immediate wrath of their supervisor and probable official disciplinary measures under the Uniform Code of Military Justice if they were anything less than discreet. So for these soldiers, discretion literally overtook valor.

Two Army aviation fuel specialists from Panama were located at the airstrip with us. They had three huge hard rubber containers of jet fuel used to refill aircraft that were shuttling supplies and personnel in and out of Matthews Ridge. The Air Force Jolly Green Giants that carried the remains of the dead Americans from Jonestown to Timheri Airport also used Matthews Ridge as a refueling point.

The fuel specialists were lower ranking than I so I was, in effect, their supervisor. One was an older soldier like Ben and me. He was very stable and was not a problem. The younger of the two was very interested in the beautiful young women of Guyana.

The Air Force set up a communications link to Jonestown and Timerhi Airport. It was manned by a young sergeant and an airman. Once our little outpost was set up and operational, these two fellows were the busiest of our bunch. They had to make sure the radio was monitored 24 hours a day. During the daylight hours, when recovery operations were being conducted, an hourly body count was transmitted to our location from Jonestown and relayed to Georgetown. We had a satellite uplink and could theoretically talk to anywhere in the world. In fact on Thanksgiving Day, we made calls home to our families. That was one of the few pleasant memories experienced in those unforgettable days.

The natives were very friendly, especially the teenaged girls with a sweet tooth for chocolates. Several American soldiers were bragging about the conquests they made and how easy it was thanks to John Wayne Bars. The aviation fuel guys would talk to the pilots while filling their helicopters and word quickly spread to Georgetown and into the halls of the Joint Task Force Command center that Brailey's guys at Matthews Ridge were getting laid for John Wayne Bars.

It was no secret that some of the men were having sexual relations with the local girls. Besides my order for discretion, they also were advised to use condoms. I had no idea that word of the extracurricular activities occurring at Matthew's Ridge among the U.S. military personnel and the local girls had reached the ears of those in high command.

One day, shortly after we arrived, an Army U21, similar to a Lear jet, landed at the airstrip. This was not unusual. Curious officers often visited from Georgetown. Most of the time, they would board a helicopter and fly into Jonestown from our strip or they would perform a cursory inspection of our site and leave as quickly as they came. We never knew when we might be visited because these officers rarely announced their itinerary.

On this morning, I believe it was the day before Thanksgiving, the 193rd Infantry Brigade Transportation officer, arrived at our air strip. She was a willowy first lieutenant with long legs and actually looked great in Army fatigues. Lieutenant Thomas was a free-spirit who enjoyed joking with the troops. This day was to be no exception.

As I saw Lieutenant Thomas descending the stairs of the small Army U21 passenger jet, I recognized who she was and decided to trot down the hill to greet her. As we approached each other, I saluted smartly. She smiled, returned my salute, then threw me the large brown distribution envelope she was carrying.

As I caught the somewhat bulky envelope, Lieutenant Thomas smiled coyly and said, "Tell your guys to have a good time on me." The envelope was full of John Wayne Bars.

Before I could think of a snappy comeback, the playful lieutenant marched back up the steps and into the waiting U21. I saw her looking at me through the aircraft's round window. Several Guyanese children were nearby, among them 15-year-old Amerindian Pauline and her friend. I opened the envelope of c-ration candy bars that Lieutenant Thomas carefully collected from the soldiers working at the airport in Georgetown and began passing the treats out to the children.

I turned around toward the U21, which had yet to begin to taxi down the runway for a take-off. The rather classy (even) sexy Lieutenant Thomas sat in the jet staring at me as I dispensed the last of the John Wayne Bars to a couple of the smaller children. I stood at attention, gave the young transportation officer a proper military salute and walked up the hill to my aid station. Her kindly deed warmed the hearts of all who witnessed this fine gesture.

A few months later, back in Panama, the 193rd Infantry Brigade was conducting a series of field training exercises at a place along the Pacific Ocean called Rio Hato. It was approximately a five hour drive from the now defunct Canal Zone. General Omar Torjillos, military ruler of the Republic of Panama had a stylish villa nearby and there was a beautiful beach just down the road.

The 601st Medical Company had the real-world mission of providing medical care for the units participating in the exercises. Since each of the three battalions in the brigade were spending 30 days training and testing in Rio Hato, one unit at a time, that meant we would be in the field there more than 90 consecutive days.

But, as mentioned earlier, Panama was the best kept secret in the Army and it was because of field duty such as this that it gained that reputation. Once our tents were set up and our clearing station was operational, there wasn't much to do but wait around for the sick and injured to arrive. Recreational activities included softball tournaments with the other units spending three months supporting the war games in Rio Hato, daily excursions to the beach, playing pinochle poker and cribbage card games, and nightly movies at the impromptu drive-in theater.

One morning, my young friend Lieutenant Thomas

reported to my Admissions and Disposition tent for sick call. She had been in Rio Hato about as long as the 601st had been set up, but this was the first time I had seen her since our encounter at the airstrip in Matthews Ridge.

"What brings you to my sick call clinic?" I asked the tall sensuous young Army officer.

"I've got a serious case of Athlete's Foot," was her reply.

I examined the lieutenant's normally pretty feet and found she was not exaggerating. The spaces between all of her toes on both feet contained ugly cracks and fissures, some that had been bleeding. The infected areas were cleansed and the appropriate antifungal cream was applied and she was given tablets to put in warm water to soak her feet in nightly. After instructing her in the proper way to use the medications and care for her feet, I escorted the pretty officer to her jeep.

Lieutenant Thomas was a flirtatious and fun-loving young lady. I had always enjoyed working with her and since we both engaged in verbal sparring and seemed to enjoy each others company, I thought it might be appropriate to ask her if she would care to join me at the nightly movie at the 601st drive-in.

"What's playing?" she asked. "'LIPSTICK' with Margo Hemmingway," I replied. "Oh, I've been wanting to see that," she said. "Then it's a date, tonight at dusk, I'll pick you up around 1815 hours (that's 6:15 PM for those of you unfamiliar with military jargon)." Obviously she had a chance to change her mind; however, she came back with, "It's a date."

Around 1600 hours (civilians, figure this one out for yourself), the company clerk came over to my tent with a message that had come in over the field phone a few minutes before. "Sorry, have to break our big date, I've got a convoy arriving at Rio Hato tonight around 1900 hrs and have to meet it. LT T."

Disappointed? Sure. I had been in Rio Hato for about three weeks and missed feminine companionship. Not that anything romantic was going to come of enjoying a movie with Lieutenant Thomas and about 100 other soldiers, but it was preferable to the nightly cribbage games with First Sergeant Arthur. Life in the military can be very unpredictable.

But, I didn't let this little adversity get me down. Without a word, I immediately went to the small refrigerator in the A&D tent normally used to store injectable antibiotics, tetanus vaccine and other medications that need to be kept cold and pulled out one of my treasured and infamous John Wayne Bars. After carefully opening the silver foil wrapper I took a small scalpel handle and attached a #15 blade. Then I skillfully operated on the candy that my men in Guyana swore was the best aphrodisiac ever made and cut it exactly in half. I meticulously rewrapped one half of the candy bar and put it in a big brown distribution envelope with a message which read:

"LT T., I cannot express how disappointed I am that you will not be able to share this evening's classic cinematic presentation with me at the only drive-in theater located within hundreds of miles. I am deeply grieved and will definitely miss your company. Please accept this small token representing my disappointment. If you promise to join me at the movies the next evening you are free, I will give you the other half. SP6 B."

Lieutenant Thomas was with me at the drive-in the next evening.

It wasn't an exaggeration that a few of our soldiers were getting sexual favors for John Wayne Bars. But rest assured, these guys would have been engaging in this extracurricular horizontal coed activity with or without chocolate candy. The explanation is elementary.

Pauline was a lovely 15-year-old Amerindian girl with a body that would make any 21-year-old woman in the United States envious. It may have been the diet or the fact that Guyanese young people are forced to walk long distances while Americans their age take the bus, or ride in a friend's car, but Pauline was one of the most physically mature teenagers imaginable.

The reader might ask how I can attest to her physical maturity. Let me assure (and perhaps disappoint) you, it wasn't because I said to Pauline one day, "Hey little girl, you want some candy?" It wasn't like that at all.

The first time I met Pauline, she and her girlfriend were wearing very thin, white cotton dresses. The sun shining through the fabric made it crystal clear that these two young ladies were wearing not one other article of clothing. Pauline was endowed with pert and ample breasts and her figure was as fine as that of any model or movie star. Her legs were equally shapely, without a trace of flab. Every inch of her skin that was visible to the eye was absolutely without blemish.

The children that would visit our site every day were made up of mainly Amerindians. I asked Pauline if she or her friends went to school. "I don't any more, the children were mean to me and my mother and father said I don't have to go back there anymore," she replied.

"Mean to you? How?" I inquired. Pauline explained that some of the bad boys would dip her pig tails in ink or cut them with scissors. She also said they would cut her dresses and she didn't have all that many dresses.

It turns out there is a great deal of racial bigotry and prejudice in Guyana against the Amerindians from the black and Indian Guyanese. The indigenous people are definitely in the minority and they are not considered as valuable as other members of the society.

Our second night at the airstrip, Sergeant Harper, a an outgoing black Guyanese Defense Force supply sergeant whom I had become friends with, asked if any of the Americans would like to "go ta town and slot some puss?"

"What's that you say?" I responded, thinking perhaps

his thick accent didn't allow me to properly interpret his words.

"Do ya wonna go ta town an' slot some puss?" Sergeant Harper again asked, in a slightly exasperated manner.

"I don't understand," I told him. As he made a circle of his left thumb and index finger and pushed his right index finger in and out of the circle several times, and repeatedly said, "slot some puss, slot some puss, slot some puss," there could be no mistaking his meaning nor the intent of his trip to town that night.

"Are there any bars in Matthews Ridge?" I asked Sergeant Harper, avoiding answering his question directly.

"Yaaaa, Mattewes Ridge got plenty bahs, mon, plenty wimen too," he laughed.

So, that night I told Fields to remain with the aid station while Sanders, Samuels, the Air Force Sergeant, one of the aviation fuel specialists and myself went to Matthews Ridge in Sergeant Harper's Land Rover. As we sped away from the GDF outpost, Sergeant Harper gave us strict instructions to all meet at the vehicle at 11 PM. That's around the time the town's electrical generator usually runs out of fuel and all the power is cut off until the morning.

Sergeant Harper took us to Mrs. Pool's Bar. Mrs. Pool was a large, happy, funny black lady with a wonderful personality. After introductions were made all around, I put an American 20 dollar bill on the bar and told Mrs. Pool to let me know when it ran out. Since a bottle of Banks Beer was $1.20, with the dollar returned when you surrendered the precious bottle (there were no bottle factories in Guyana at the time), we managed to drink all night and Mrs Pool didn't ask for anymore money.

As I was sitting at the bar talking to Sergeant Harper and Mrs. Pool about their town and country, my little friend Pauline stuck her head in the doorway. I motioned for her to come in and join us, since there were many other children in the bar that were her age and younger, but she simply replied, "I cannot." and kept watching us.

I again tried to verbally coax her in and again she simply replied, "I cannot."

I told her I would come out and sit on the porch with her and asked what she would like to drink, thinking she would respond with, "orange" or some other soft drink. "I'll have a Banks please and one for my brother Frank." was her reply.

"You are too young to drink beer," I said emphatically to this 15-year-old Amerindian girl.

"I am not!" was her equally firm and defiant reply.

I looked to Mrs. Pool and Sergeant Harper for guidance and they both indicated that it was no problem for Pauline and her 17-year-old brother Frank to drink a Banks Beer. So Mrs. Pool opened three frosty bottles of Banks and I carried them out to the porch, where the three of us sat and talked. Frank and Pauline told me that Mrs. Pool would not allow Amerindians into her bar. It was then I realized all the children and patrons in the bar were black.

I learned that Frank was the oldest of 13 children his mother and father brought into the world. His father worked for the government and was away, but all of the children were at home. Pauline asked if I would like to meet her mother and other brothers and sisters. I told her I didn't want to impose, but both she and Frank said her mother has been talking about the Americans and wanted to meet one of the visitors.

I asked how far away their house was, and Pauline

answered, “Just up the ridge a bit.” Frank said he had some place else to go to. I told Sergeant Harper and the others that Pauline wanted me to meet her family. The GDF supply sergeant reminded me of the 11 PM deadline for the return trip to the airstrip, three miles away.

We began trudging up the fairly steep rocky incline for which the town is named. Breathing quickly became very difficult. Although Pauline’s family lived less than a mile from Mrs. Pool’s bar, it felt more like climbing Mount Everest. By the time we finally reached the home, my legs ached fiercely and I was drenched in perspiration. Young Pauline appeared as fresh as when she did before we began the trek.

Her mother was very nice. She was probably only a couple of years older than me yet she seemed tired... or shy... perhaps both. No doubt raising a dozen plus one children had something to do with that. Pauline’s mother served tea and I met all of the other younger children. I also met Pauline’s grandfather. The home was very simple, the walls white washed and very clean inside and out. The hot tea was refreshing and we had a pleasant visit.

At about 10:30 PM, I checked my pocket watch and said it was time for me to go. I always wore a pocket watch when assigned to tropical countries because I've never been able to find a wrist watch band that would not give me a rash after a few days in the heat and humidity.

"That's a fine pocket watch," Pauline's grandfather said of the small timepiece that cost less than 10 dollars in a PX in Panama. "Would you like it?" I asked the old man, hoping the watch could serve as a small token of gratitude for the hospitality I had enjoyed that evening.

"Oh, I couldn't take such a fine gift," he said. I insisted and said I had another one and wouldn't miss this one. He asked if there was anything I wanted from Guyana. I said that the country's stamps were unusually beautiful. "My daughter collects stamps and would love some canceled ones from your country," was my response. For the next several years the old man would send us a box of canceled Guyanese stamps at around Christmas time.

My engaging conversation with the grandfather had taken up too much time and I was anxious to catch up with Sergeant Harper and the rest of the team. The last thing my aching legs were looking forward to was a three mile march to the airfield. As Pauline and I left her house for the less strenuous walk down the ridge, the power suddenly went off, cloaking the entire town in instant darkness. Kerosene lanterns began to appear in some windows causing eerie shadows to appear on this moonless night. I said to Pauline, "I thought the power went off at 11 PM." "It goes off when there's no more petrol," she simply.

We continued down the ridge and to my distress, the next sound I heard was Sergeant Harper's Land Rover starting up. We were at least a quarter of a mile away and I knew that meant I was in for a long walk in the pitch dark conditions down an unfamiliar dirt road, in a strange country. I told Pauline I wasn't relishing the hike. Just then we passed a two story building with kerosene lanterns in each window. "Do you want to go in here?" Pauline asked, pointing to the building. "What is that building?" I asked her. "It's the hotel," was Pauline's short reply. Matthews Ridge only hotel was a very modest two story seven room building.

I told Pauline that I could not stay in town tonight because I had responsibilities at the airstrip and would hike back there. She took my hand caressingly and said, "I don't mean for the whole night."

I was dumbfounded. "Pauline!" I almost shouted, retrieving my hand, "You are only 15-years-old!"

"I may be 15 years old, but in Guyana I am a woman!" was the sharp and hurt reply I will never forget.

As we stood there in the dark, outside the only hotel in Matthews Ridge, I tried to explain to Pauline that in America, 30-year-old men do not make love with children half their age. This woman-child, with a body as sexually appealing as any I'd ever seen, was extremely offended. She turned in a huff and before I knew it, disappeared into the dark tropical night.

I found my way back to the airstrip with the help of a friendly Guyanese man who offered to accompany me on my walk in the dark. When I had told him I could get back by myself. He said there were snakes that come out at night and can kill you if they strike. Thinking he might be trying to set me up for a mugging or worse, I pointed to the .45 strapped on my pistol belt. He said, I will not be able to tell the snakes are there and I decided to take my chance with the seemingly friendly man, rather than the alleged deadly snakes.

We arrived at the airstrip aid station without mishap and I insisted my Guyanese good Samaritan take four c-ration meals for his trouble. When he looked at the contents of one box, he shook my hand vigorously and thanked me profusely. "This box will feed my family for one meal," he solemnly stated after inspecting its contents.

The next morning, when I related my experience with Pauline in front of Matthews Ridges's only hotel, to Sergeant Harper, he laughed and said she was right, I should have gone to bed with her. He told me she wasn't a virgin and I would not have been disappointed. He also said that girls in this frontier region were encouraged to have babies because there was a border dispute with Venezuela to the west and the Guyanese government felt a larger local population would lend justification and legitimacy to their claims, even if the legitimacy of the children was in question.

The U.S. military had journeyed to a strange country on an unreal mission; a place where adolescent girls are encouraged to make babies, beer bottles cost five times what their contents does, and the children have never eaten chocolate. Compared to some of the other events I was to experience during my extended week in Guyana, these things now don't seem so strange after all.

Five

"I don't want to go down there"

On November 20th, when Captain Snow and Major Buenos returned from their short visit to Jonestown, the brigade surgeon instructed me to gather up enough anti-malaria drugs for the 100 or so American soldiers who were scheduled to arrive there later that day or early the next. I quickly assembled a kit full of drugs and told Major Buenos it was ready. The assignment was to get me aboard the GDF helicopter and fly to Jonestown and make sure the medications were properly distributed to all of the troops.

When I had first learned my aid station was to be set up at Matthews Ridge, some 20 miles from the carnage in Jonestown, I was relieved. No one would desire to work around the remains of all those people who had been killed on Saturday. Now, I tried to convince Major Buenos to allow me to send Ben Samuels or Rick Fields to perform this relatively simple task.

"No," Major Buenos said, "Specialist Brailey, you are the senior medic, you will go."

As I gathered my personal gear and the drug kit and walked toward the waiting helicopter, a light rain began to fall from the gray overcast sky. It was the dry season, but this was inland, near the tropical rain forests, and "dry" doesn't mean the same as it does on the coast where Georgetown is located.

The awaiting helicopter was a Bell 310 that the U.S. Army calls a UH1 or "Huey." After saluting the GDF pilots in the traditional palm-down American style, it was interesting to note that they responded with the British palm-up salute, a reminder that this country was once a colony of Great Britain. The chopper was void of seats, just as was the Guyanese airliner that brought our team to Matthews Ridge was.

The pilot informed me we would be taking off momentarily, as soon as supplies for the GDF troops guarding Jonestown arrived. Within minutes, a battered civilian truck pulled up next to the helicopter. Two large, whole, unwrapped fish were deposited on the floor of the aircraft, along with a large bag of rice and some fresh vegetables.

I jumped into the back of the helicopter with the cargo as the pilot and co-pilot took their positions in the front. Thankfully, they offered me a helmet equipped with a microphone and ear pieces so we three could communicate during the short 20 mile flight. The chopper was cranked up and following the engine run-up, we were airborne, heading toward a place with more dead human bodies scattered about than any other place I had ever been including Vietnam. There were undoubtedly more newly dead, unprocessed human remains in Jonestown that morning than in any other place on earth.

The rain was still falling steadily and it wasn't long before the chopper entered the thick bank of clouds that was creating the rainfall. Speeding through those clouds in that aircraft felt a lot like riding in a car through a thick fog at 100 miles an hour. It was impossible to see anything beyond the helicopter itself. It was equipped with radar and a seemingly workable altimeter, so there was little danger of hitting a tree or a mountain or being hit by another aircraft, hopefully!

I questioned as to why GDF choppers were painted a bright international orange, as opposed to the traditional dark olive drab color of the U.S. Army's machines. The pilot responded by saying, "Easier to find them when they crash in the jungle." Very logical, but not very reassuring to a passenger taking his first ride in a GDF helicopter, even if it was made in the USA.

Within a few minutes we had arrived over Jonestown and began our descent from the gloomy clouds. It was comforting to once again be able to see the ground. We were about 1000 feet over the commune when we broke through the clouds.

"Where are all the bodies?" I asked, trying to sound as self-assured and confident as possible. "Right down there mate," was the co-pilot's answer.

I told the pilot and co-pilot that it was difficult to make out the bodies from this great height and before I finished getting the words out of my mouth, the blaze orange GDF helicopter made a rapid spiral descent to about 150 feet over what we learned was called the "Pavilion."

From this elevation, what had appeared to be multicolored piles of trash in a landfill from 1000 feet were easily recognized as masses of bodies in various colors of clothing. Arms and legs were extended from bodies so bloated the formerly loose fitting shirts, and trousers that are so comfortable to wear in the tropics, were tight against the gas-filled bodies of their wearers. Even the severe prop wash of the helicopter hovering overhead did not make the taut cloth flutter in the powerful rotor blast.

It looked like the scene from a macabre horror film, but the people laying below were not mannequins set out by some Hollywood set designer, nor were they movie extras in make up who would rise and walk away when the director called "Cut!" They were the quickly rotting remains of dead humans: men, women and children; who until a few short days ago, had been living, breathing beings with dreams and aspirations that probably were not too different from our own. It was determined that for the past year or more, most of them had been living a miserable existence, but at least where there is life there is hope. There was no hope left in Jonestown, only horror, and I said aloud to no one in particular, "I don't want to go down there."

"Don't blame you," was the curt reply of the pilot.

Within a minute or so, we were landing in a large open expanse that was to be known as the Soccer Field. The Guyanese probably called it a "football" field. At this moment, this was the only aircraft on the ground in Jonestown, but within a day, this field would become the busiest airport in the country of Guyana as American soldiers and supplies were brought in and the remains of the dead Jonestown resident were removed.

It was a relief to disembark from that small helicopter. The short ride through the dark rain-filled clouds had been disorienting, the unfamiliar and pungent odor of the fish was not pleasant and I had to sit on my haunches in that seatless aircraft to avoid their natural juices from soaking my fatigue trousers whenever the helicopter turned or pitched. The spiral maneuvers that positioned us over the mass of bodies around the pavilion also caused my stomach to churn uncontrollably.

But the smell of the fish was exotic perfume compared to the awful odor that invaded my nostrils when the chopper landed and its hatch was slid open. The dead bodies had been laying in the sweltering Jonestown heat for nearly three days at that point. The temperature during the day had been nearly 100 degrees on Sunday. It was the same on this dismal Monday, despite the rain. If you haven't experienced the awful odor emitted from more than 900 dead and rotting bodies laying in close proximity to one another, there is no way it can adequately be described. The best description I can give, and it is an admittedly most inadequate one, is that it is a sickeningly sweet, overpowering scent. Nothing but time will rid the senses of it. The odor permeates one's skin and clothing and after having been exposed to it for any length of time, it seems impossible to wash the smell from your body and it is impossible to remove it from your clothes and equipment. They all have to be discarded and burned or buried.

Some of the Guyanese soldiers at the soccer field that day were wearing kerchiefs over their mouths and noses. I tried it and it had no affect whatsoever in lessening the intensity of the disgusting odor. It only added to the claustrophobic feeling of being smothered by the smell as well as the kerchief every time you took in a breath of that putrid air. When the rest of the American soldiers arrived, some of them tried wearing their protective (gas) masks. The strong smell even permeated the filters of those masks made to protect soldiers from the effects of poison gases and biological agents.

I looked around at the uniforms and faces of the living people I saw in Jonestown. Some of the GDF troops removed their rations from the floor of the helicopter. No one was wearing an American uniform, nor did I spot anyone who appeared to be anything but a Guyanese citizen. A GDF lieutenant approached me and we exchanged salutes. His name was Lieutenant Abbott. He was the commander of the 20 or so GDF troops who had been guarding Jonestown since the morning before.

Lieutenant Abbott seemed tired and drawn. His emotional affect was flat. He appeared to be suffering what World War I soldiers called "Shell Shock," World War II and Korean War veterans described as "combat fatigue," or what those of us who served in Vietnam came to know as post-traumatic-stress syndrome.

"I don't want to go down there"

"Are you alright, Lieutenant?" I asked. "What... oh, yes... Just haven't slept since I don't know when... none of us have... difficult to sleep here..." was his disjointed reply.

The haggard young officer then asked if I was the medic Major Buenos told him would be coming. I said I was and he told me that no members of the American task force had arrived yet, but the first flight was expected any time now. "In the meantime," he asked, "would you like a tour of Jonestown?" I told him I would. I didn't realize what I was getting myself into.

From where I stood at the edge of the soccer field, rows of neat wooden cottages on short stilts could be easily seen. They appeared to be freshly painted, mostly bright blue with red trim, but some were a clean, bright white. The open-air pavilion was about 100 yards away. It had a tin roof as did most of the buildings and even the most gentle rain played the tin like a drum. The Pavilion was held up by bark-trimmed logs and there were crossbeams made of timber. The logs were painted brown and the crossbeams were white. Most of the bodies were in or near the pavilion.

Wooden walkways led from the pavilion to two buildings about the same distance away from I as we were. They both were painted white. It was pointed out that these were Rev. Jim Jones' house and the infirmary. A high garage-like metal building containing at least one tractor with a flat bed trailer attached to it, was near the soccer field.

Lieutenant Abbott beckoned me to follow him. It was obvious by the intent in his step that he had an itinerary for my tour worked out in his tired mind. As we passed rows of stilted cottages with neatly manicured yards, a few bodies were strewn here and there, not in large groups, but singly and in twos or threes. They looked not unlike dolls that little girls had thrown aside after tiring of playing with them.

Abbott approached the open doorway of one of the cottages on the edge of the jungle. He ordered me inside in a voice that seemed more resolute and stern than his previous one. In the stifling one-room cabin, I saw several bodies, each had obviously been shot at close range with a heavy-gauge shot gun. They were all of the black race.

"I brought you here first because I wanted to show you Americans were the only ones to die here. These are my countrymen. They were shot - murdered," the lieutenant stated matter-of-factly.

I asked what so many Guyanese were doing in the American commune of Jonestown. Abbott said he wasn't sure. He thought some of them worked here and some were family members of those that did. He felt others might have been visitors who chose a most inopportune time to visit Jonestown.

The next stop was the commune's radio tower. We ascended the vertical wooden ladder and entered the platform. A lone white victim of the mass suicide lay on the floor, a pad and pencil in his hand. The unknown man had taken the poisonous brew and apparently began recording his reaction to it. After three short paragraphs, this man's final thoughts and feelings became illegible as the convulsive effects of the cyanide overtook him.

Climbing down from the tower, Lieutenant Abbot proceeded to take me to Jones' house. Although I had never seen pictures of the man in life, in death he appeared to be a leader and the strikingly strange position of his body caused me to imagine what must have been going through his mind immediately before his death.

Jones was laying face up, reclined on the three or

four steps leading into the front doorway of his house. Unlike the death photos of this madman that appeared in American news magazines of the day showing one arm bent over his head and the other above him lying on the stairs, when I saw Jones on November 20, his arms were both extended into the air, locked in place by rigor mortis. His eyes were open and he seemed to be arguing with the God he denied until the very moment he died.

A bullet hole was on one side of his forehead. There was a little blood around the hole. I didn't move the body, but I did not notice any pools of blood in the area back of his head indicating an exit wound. I specifically looked for powder burns or residue around the wound on his temple and there were none, indicating that Jones had been murdered and did not commit suicide as was later reported by the U.S. Government and the media.

The lieutenant stepped up into Jones' house, carefully avoiding touching the body of this fallen would-be messiah. I did the same. Laying in front of an open, empty safe was a woman, also shot. I believe this was Annie Moore. On the bed in a room to the right was another dead woman. She was laying on her back with no apparent wounds. I believe this was the remains of Maria Katsaris.

By this time, the stench of the dead and the enormity of the carnage was beyond description. My stomach was in a sorry state, ready to expel its meager contents and definitely not ready to replace it any time soon. My head was swimming. Although the odor was no better outside the house, I had to escape its confines and put my face into the light breeze that was wafting through the commune. The rain had ceased, but the dark overcast indicated it could begin again at any time.

Our next stop on this bizarre tour of the "City of the Not-So-Long Dead" known as Jonestown was the infirmary. Empty pill bottles and injection vials littered its otherwise clean floor. Many of the identifying labels showed they had contained psychotropic drugs I was familiar with. Librium, Valium, and Sodium Phenobarbital were prominent among them.

The clinic boasted a modern x-ray machine and a training microscope with two eye pieces. Other instruments and pieces of medical equipment were equally modern. There were no bodies in the infirmary, but Lieutenant Abbott, knowing I was a medic, felt I would be interested in seeing it. I took note of Dr. Larry Schact's medical degree on the wall and I wondered out loud how someone who studied for years to become a healer could have been an integral part of this gross insult to humanity and decency. Lieutenant Abbot did not reply.

As we were walking toward the pavilion where the main mass of fallen residents of Jonestown were located, the unmistakable sound of incoming Jolly Green Giant helicopters could be heard in the distance. "That must be your comrades," said Lieutenant Abbott. "Shall we continue?" "Yes," I replied flatly.

I noticed many of the bodies seemed to be laying in family groups and several dozen of them wore hand-made identification bracelets fashioned of paper and transparent tape. By this time, the bodies were so bloated that the bracelets were actually imbedded in their skin.

A few minutes after the first Jolly Green Giant helicopters landed and shut their engines down, Lieutenant Abbott and I concluded our tour. I had seen Jim Jones, apparently pleading to the God he defied and rejected until the end. I saw his wooden throne with the sign over it reading, "Those who forget the past are destined to repeat it. Santayana" I saw the pot of bubbling purple brew, made from Fla-Vor-Ade, not the Kool-Ade erroneously reported by the media. The deadly poison contained in it had been forced down the throats of babies and children with needle-less syringes by the very mothers who had given them life. The syringes were littered all around.

I saw dead dogs and a large dead chimpanzee that had been shot and killed. I wondered why all these animals were killed and yet two beautiful blue macaws sitting on their perches were not. Perhaps the masters of the dead animals wanted to be reunited with their pets in that great hereafter wherever they believed their eternal souls would be directed to. Perhaps the birds were allowed to live so they could bear witness to the insanity that struck Jonestown on November 18, 1978. But if that was thereason they were spared, these parrots weren't talking.

I had seen what Lieutenant Abbott wanted me to see so he could satisfy himself that he did what he could so the world would know Americans weren't the only ones to die in Jonestown. I had seen what I needed to see so that I could someday report to the world what happened in this place. I had seen far far more than I desired to see.

Even worse, I had seen far more than I'll ever be able to forget.

When we arrived back at the soccer field, two of the U.S. Special Forces troops who had arrived in the helicopters had already managed to start the engine of the tractor with the flat bed trailer and it was being used to move bundles of plastic, brownish-black body bags from the Jolly Green Giants to an area near the pavilion. I approached another Special Forces soldier that I knew from Panama, a medic. I gave him all the malaria medication and instructed him to insure all American personnel working in Jonestown receive their proper doses.

Some of the soldiers who had come in on the helicopters were from the Graves Registration Company at Fort Lee, Virginia. There were around two dozen of them clustered around an officer, apparently being briefed on how this difficult mission was to be accomplished. The soldiers from the States coordinated with the well trained and highly disciplined Special Forces troops from Panama. Although they appeared to be typical American soldiers, it takes a special breed of person to carry out the indescribably difficult mission given the Graves Registration personnel. They surely are unsung heroes! Pray tell, what would they look like when the mission was over, days from now?

Lieutenant Abbott told me the helicopter I had arrived in would return shortly, bringing fresh GDF troops to relieve his tired men. He asked if I was ready to go back to Matthews Ridge. I told the young Guyanese officer that I had been ready from he moment I first set foot on the ground in Jonestown. He managed to give me a weak but genuine smile of understanding.

The GDF helicopter landed and eight new soldiers, in clean, freshly pressed uniforms disembarked from it, while eight of their tired counterparts in sweat-stained clothing, who had the grim task of being the first group to guard the dead of Jonestown for the past nearly 36 hours, eagerly prepared to load out. There were no noisy greetings exchanged between the incoming and outgoing groups, as was the custom of American soldiers performing similar changes. Instead you could see signs of fear and trepidation on the faces of those just arriving and relief on those that were leaving. I gratefully joined this group as did a small nervous Caucasian American in a white short-sleeved shirt and dress slacks. He was carrying a wooden crate with no top. It was filled to overflowing with documents.

"Is that thing loaded?" asked my jittery countryman as he pointed to the .45 on my pistol belt.

"Of course it is," was my reply.

"If anybody tries to take this box away from me, shoot them," he ordered softly and seriously as he stepped aboard the helicopter.

"You've got to be kidding," I responded incredulously. "No I am not," he answered flatly.

"Look buddy," I said to the little American civilian with a seriousness that at least equalled his, "I don't know who you are and I don't know what you've got in that box, but whatever it is, there is no way I am going to risk spending even one day in a Guyanese jail because I shot someone trying to take that box away from you."

We sat next to each other on the floor of the helicopter as the tired Guyanese sentries found space to sit. These eight young GDF troopers had been the only living beings outnumbered by more than100 to 1 by the dead residents of Jonestown for a day and a half. They were exhausted and did not display the least bit interest in the conversation I was having with the weird American bureaucrat or in the box he was sheltering between his legs.

"I'm from the U.S. Embassy in Georgetown," my mysterious associate informed me, "I've been here since yesterday gathering up these documents. They are very sensitive. We can't let them get into the wrong hands," he told me in a forceful, yet panicky voice.

"Let me make this very clear to you sir," I said to the State Department man, "I don't care if you are President Jimmy Carter himself. This weapon is for my personal protection and unless I feel my life is in danger, I'm not going to use it.

"Give it to me then," he half ordered and half begged in a tentative squeaky voice, genuine fear showing in his bloodshot eyes when he removed his sunshades so he could see in the whithering sunlight.

"Listen, I don't know you and I don't like you. This .45 is going to remain in its holster and if anyone draws it out it is going to be me and if you keep f***ing with me it will be to shoot you!" I yelled at this American whose sanity I was very unsure of at the moment.

About the same time I was shouting at the State Department guy, the pilot started the engine of the Bell 300. Attempting further conversation would have been difficult at best over the roar of its powerful engine, even if we chose to converse. For once in my military career, the loud noise of the helicopter was welcome because it relieved me of the ability to communicate with this strange dude from the embassy.

Although darkness was approaching, it was obvious that the helicopter was flying in the opposite direction of Matthews Ridge. “Where are we going?” I shouted into one of the GDF troopers' ear. “Port Kaitumba,” was the answer he fired back at me.

Port Kaitumba was the place where Congressman Ryan, four journalists and a defector were murdered a little more than 48 hours before. We landed within a few minutes of our departure from Jonestown. As the weary GDF troopers emptied out of the helicopter, the two yellow and white Guyana Airways planes Ryan and his ill-fated entourage were to fly out on were parked at the edge of the short runway. Numerous bullet holes appeared as black spots on the aircraft's skin in the quickly waning daylight.

Later I learned the mission of Jones' confidante, Larry Layton and his impromptu assassination squad. They had planned to board the aircraft and force the pilots to take off. Once the planes were high in the air, a gunman on each plane was to kill the pilot, causing both of the small airplanes and their passengers to crash into the jungle and perish. The plan was botched when one of the gunmen, perhaps unwilling to sacrifice his life, entered one of the planes and began shooting. No one can say with any degree of certainty what actually took place that fateful day, but this action was the catalyst that finally caused Rev. Jim Jones to direct his flock to take their own lives.

On the Port Kaitumba to Matthews Ridge leg of this short bizarre journey, the U.S. Embassy man and I were the only passengers. By now, the total darkness of the night enveloped us and I sat on the opposite side of the helicopter from this odd nervous American, trying to keep as much space between him and I as possible. I regarded him as one might a weird off-the-wall relative who one doesn't want to be seen in public with or appear to be related.

When we landed at the Matthews Ridge airstrip, Captain Snow and Major Buenos stood waiting to board the chopper, whose next destination was Timheri Airport, some 150 miles away. As the door slid open and I jumped out, Captain Snow approached me.

"How'd it go," he yelled in my ear over the din of the waiting helicopter. "Mission accomplished," I replied curtly. "Are you leaving?" I asked.

"Yeah, Major Buenos and I are going back to Georgetown. We'll work out of there. You've got everything under control here. Call us if you need anything," Snow shouted over the noise of the chopper.

"Watch out for that little guy on the helicopter," I warned the Captain, "he's some kind of CIA spook or something. Wanted me to shoot anyone who tried to take his damn box away from him."

Captain Snow did not reply. Perhaps because I referred to the other passenger's diminutive stature and it made him more self conscious of his own, or maybe Snow knew something I didn't. At any rate, he turned toward the helicopter, staring at the State Department man intently as Major Buenos got in, then Snow shook his head back and forth and he got into the helicopter.

I watched the GDF bird lift into the starless night until it's running lights disappeared from view. Then I strolled slowly up the hill to our aid station, hoping one of the guys was thoughtful enough to set up my cot and lay out my sleeping bag. They were. I never saw the man from the U.S. Embassy again and I never learned his name or what his function was.

Monday, November 20, 1978 had been one of the most bizarre days of my life, but the real weirdness was just beginning. The next eight days would test the credulity and strain the sanity of many of the Americans performing this very strange and most unmilitary mission.

> "Death is the king of this world: 'tis his park where he breeds life to feed him. Cries of pain are music for his banquet." **George Eliot**

> "Kill one man and you are a murderer. Kill millions and you are a conqueror. Kill everyone and you are a God." **Jean Rostand**

Six

Graves Registration

It is the summer of 1998 as this is being written. The term "Graves Registration" has been replaced by "Mortuary Affairs." Currently, the 54th Quartermaster Company of Fort Lee Virginia is the only mortuary affairs unit on a active duty in the United States Army. It is due to the relative peace our world enjoys and the fact that the military of the United States is serving to keep the peace rather than engaging in conflict that has allowed the Army to reduce the manpower dedicated to the search, recovery, processing and evacuation of the remains and personal effects of U.S. soldiers, airmen, seamen and marines who have fallen in combat.

The U.S. Army Quartermaster Corps last supported mortuary affairs operations during combat conditions in Panama during "Operation Just Cause" and in the Gulf War. It also provided support in Somalia, Haiti and Bosnia. In 1995, sixteen soldiers from the 54th QM Company deployed to Oklahoma City, Oklahoma to provide assistance to that state's Medical Examiner's Office in recovering and evacuating the fatalities that resulted from the April 1995 bombing of the Federal Building there. That marked the first time the unit had been called on to support a mass fatality operation within the United States.

On December 12, 1985, a chartered DC-8 crashed shortly after taking off from an airport near Gander, Newfoundland. It had just refueled. Two-hundred-and-forty-eight soldiers from the 101st Airborne Division returning home from a six-month peace-keeping mission in the Sinai Desert perished in the crash. The wreckage of the aircraft along with the badly burned and dismembered bodies of its passengers and crew were strewn over a three-quarter of a mile area of thick frozen forest.

Less than 24 hours after the crash, a special Graves Registration (GRREG) Search and Recovery Team from the Quartermaster Center at Fort Lee, Virginia arrived in Newfoundland to assist Canadian officials. Joined by other military and civilian personnel, for weeks, the GRREG team combed and sifted every square foot of the crash site, searching for the remains of victims and their personal effects. All items found were noted, sorted, characterized and reconciled to one another as appropriate. In the end, despite the severe damage caused by the incredibly violent crash and fire and the remote location in which it occurred, all of the deceased were properly identified and accorded a proper burial.

Dr. Steven E. Anders, a physician who serves as the historian for the U.S. Army Quartermaster General, wrote an excellent history of the Quartermaster's Graves Registration mission that appeared in the Quartermaster Professional Bulletin of September 1988. It provides the best chronology of the development of mortuary affairs as it exists in the U.S. Army today.

During the early 1800's, it was the Quartermaster officers, the storekeepers of the Army, who cared for the dead. There wasn't any regulation assigning them this important job, it apparently became their responsibility because "someone had to do it." These officers, assigned to the forts along our young country's frontier, constructed cemetery plots, buried the dead in marked graves and kept a fairly uniform record of burial. This was acceptable, as long as the Army stayed near the fort and was not in some far away region of the territory. The practical experience these officers received and the methods they devised in no way prepared them for the challenge of handling massive combat fatalities resulting from a large-scale conflict. At that point in our nation's history, its military had not even thought to address a formal policy to react to that contingency.

The Mexican War of 1846 to 1847 changed all that by providing the Army's first real test to care for its war dead. To put it bluntly, it failed the test miserably. General Zachary Taylor insured the dead were properly collected and buried on the battlefield following his victory at Buena Vista. However, he neglected to mark the site of the graves on his official report. The locations of those long lost makeshift cemeteries containing those Americans who fell in the Battle of Buena Vista have never been found.

During the same war, General Winfield Scott landed troops at Vera Cruz and marched them to Mexico City. Hundreds of American soldiers died and were buried along the march route. Only a few dozen of the graves were ever located after the war and none of the remains laying in them were ever identified.

With the U.S. Civil War came the foundation of the Army's Grave Registration mission. This one conflict caused more combat casualties and accounted for more battlefield deaths than all of the nation's other major wars combined. The public expressed a greater concern for the soldiers on both sides who were fighting this war, perhaps it is because it was fought where they lived.

While concern for the dead was evident during the Civil War, the methods of burial did not immediately change. The dead, on both sides, were almost always buried by details of soldiers chosen at random. The graves were dug at or very near the scene of the battle. After the armies left, the temporary markers identifying the grave sites and remains were left to deteriorate, leaving little chance for family members to locate the exact resting places of loved ones.

Another problem that contributed to the proper identification of remains buried after a battle was that often, prisoners-of-war made up the burial details. These captured enemy soldiers were somewhat less than motivated to accurately and permanently mark the grave sites of their enemies. Often the POWs were illiterate and could not properly mark the graves despite the best of intentions. During the fighting at the Wilderness and Spotsylvania Courthouse, around 1500 soldiers were killed. Less than 400 graves were ever later identified.

On May 4, 1864, when the Union Army of the Potomac crossed the Rapidan River and entered Virginia, the soldiers were horrified to find the bleached bones of others who wore the blue in battle the year before, lying exposed on the ground. Many of the grief-filled soldiers methodically searched through the remains hoping to discover clues that would provide positive identification of fallen friends. They searched for marks on clothing and equipment, evidence of fatal wounds and peculiarities of tooth structure during their often futile quests. These methods of identifying the remains of the dead would become part of the standard operating procedures for GRREG soldiers in the 20th century.

Finally, before moving into the wilderness, the living troops who were concerned about their dead comrades, took time to bury their remains. The fear of being an "unknown" soldier was constantly on the minds of combat troops in the Civil War. While the War Department had yet to even think of issuing identification tags to its troops, many of them began carrying items on their persons to ensure they would be accurately identified should they fall mortally wounded on the field of battle.

Many soldiers carried identifying markers fashioned from wood. Others wore medallions around their necks that bore their names and other identifying information. Prior to attacking the Confederates at Mine Run in the winter of 1863, the men of the Union Army's Fifth Corps wrote their names on pieces of paper and pinned them to their uniforms. Despite these individual unofficial efforts, the remains of only about 58 percent of the soldiers who died in the Civil War were ever positively identified.

The U.S. Army establishment of that day did not appreciate the need for some form of permanent identification for combatants, nor did it understand the obvious need for specially trained units and personnel who could properly care for war dead. Only once during the Civil War, after the Battle of Fort Stevens outside of Washington, DC in the summer of 1864, did a group similar to the modern GRREG unit come into being. Captain James M. Moore, the newly appointed commander of the Quartermaster Cemeterial Division took a group of his personnel to the site of the fighting after the battle ended. For the first time in history, Moore's team systematically searched for and recorded the remains and personal effects of all fallen soldiers and was able to positively identify everyone that had been killed.

While it took decades for subsequent GRREG units to match the accomplishment of Captain Moore's team, the Civil War did motivate the Army to clearly designate the Quartermaster Corps as the official entity responsible for caring for war dead. Between 1866 and 1870, the Cemeterial Division transferred the remains of almost 300,000 soldiers to 73 newly created national cemeteries.

Almost three-and-a-half decades after the Civil War, during the Spanish-American War, Graves Registration was to become more professional. As a result of experiences in Cuba, it was learned that successful identification of remains depended mostly on shortening the time span between death, original burial and registration of graves. Chaplain Charles C. Pierce, who established the Quartermaster Office of Identification in the Philippines formalized some of the basic principles and techniques needed to identify war dead. He recommended the wearing of an "identity disc" by soldiers and the establishment of collection points where mortuary records could be gathered, filed, checked and corrected.

In 1913, new regulations establishing a firm commitment by the U.S. Army to positively identify and bury all war dead. It became required to file detailed maps of all grave sites at the time of initial burial to make the process of disinternment more efficient. By 1917, the War Department required all combat soldiers to wear identification (dog) tags.

General Pershing requested establishment of the first Graves Registration Service during World War I. Chaplain Pierce, by then long retired from military service, was recalled to duty two decades after his establishment of the Office of Identification in Manila, to train GRREG troops and units at the Philadelphia Quartermaster Depot.

By October 1917, Pierce's headquarters was moved to Tours, France, from where 19 Quartermaster GRREG companies were dispatched to every section of the combat zone.

While the headquarters of the Graves Registration Service consolidated and preserved mortuary records and maintained cemeteries at the rear of the battlefield, the GRREG companies supported the troops on the line. The dedication and espirit de corps of these soldiers, whose mission was to care for those comrades who had eternally lost their capability to soldier any longer, was extraordinary. These men often took incredibly dangerous risks in their efforts to insure proper identification of fellow soldiers who had fallen. General Pershing wrote about one unit in the spring of 1918:

"(They) began their work under heavy shell of fire and gas, and, although troops were in dugouts, these men immediately went to the cemetery and in order to preserve records and locations, repaired and erected new crosses as fast as the old ones were blown down. They also completed extension of the cemetery, this work occupying a period of one and a half hours, during which time shells

were falling continuously and they were subjected to mustard gas. They gathered many bodies which had first been in the hands of the Germans, and were later retaken by American counterattacks. Identification was especially difficult, all papers and tags have been removed, and most of the bodies, being in a terrible condition and beyond recognition."

During World War I, the relatives of fallen U.S. servicemen agreed to have the remains of their loved ones interned in the country where they had fallen. President Theodore Roosevelt encouraged this alternative by requesting that his son, Quentin, be buried near the ground where he was killed. "Where the tree falls, let it lie," were the poetic words Roosevelt used as did many other grieving American families.

Eight cemeteries had been established in Europe by the end of World War I. Six were in France, one in Belgium and one in Britain. Approximately 30,000 of America's dead from that war are buried in those cemeteries. Over 47,000 bodies were returned to the United States for reburial after World War I.

During The Great War, the percentage of unknown remains was around three per hundred bodies recovered. This still was not acceptable to the families of the nearly 2400 men who perished during World War I and were never identified. But Graves Registration was becoming scientific and systematized. Future conflicts would challenge the talents, perserverence and ingenuity of the GRREG personnel in ways they have never been challenged.

More than 250,000 Americans died and were buried in temporary cemeteries around the world during World War II. On the continent of Europe alone, the remains were interned over a million-and-a-half square miles, making the recovery process extremely difficult. Newer and more devastating weapons often made many of those killed in combat unrecognizable.

A Graves Registration Company in World War II consisted of 260 enlisted men and five officers to support three combat divisions. One platoon was assigned per division and each platoon had two sections, a collecting squad and an evacuation squad. These companies collected, evacuated, identified and supervised the burial of the dead. They also collected and properly disposed of personal effects and selected sites for temporary cemeteries.

The work performed by the GRREG teams in World War II was just as hazardous and stressful as that done by their predecessors in World War I, if not more so. During the fierce battle for Anzio, graves registration troops were forced to take shelter in freshly dug graves. During the D-Day Invasion, men from the Graves Registration company who were with the First Army, gathered bodies from the beaches, ocean and inland, actually extricating them from submerged landing craft. By the end of the second day of the invasion, one platoon had buried 457 dead American servicemen.

After World War II, most graves registration units were disbanded and most overseas GRREG services ceased to exist. This created an enormous problem in June of 1950 when war broke out in Korea. Only the 108th Graves Registration Platoon in Yokohama, Japan was available to deploy to Korea during the emergency buildup. The platoon consisted of 30 men, most of who were without combat experience.

Other GRREG personnel were rounded up from the 565th Quartermaster Graves Registration Company at

Fort Bragg, North Carolina. Five men were attached to the three combat divisions deployed to Korea, the 24th, 25th and 1st Cavalry. They were ill-supplied. The fluid tactical situation made recovery of remains extremely difficult. A centrally located Army cemetery could not be set up so separate divisional -level cemeteries were established instead.

In the fall of 1950, these cemeteries were forced to be quickly closed down due to a renewed and intense communist offensive. The dead were then evacuated to secure rear areas then sent to Japan from processing and subsequent shipment to the United States. This was the first time in U.S. history that a mass evacuation of combat dead took place while hostilities were still being conducted. By the end of January 1951, nearly 5,000 bodies had been removed from temporary cemeteries in Korea to a newly formed central identification unit (CIU) in Japan.

By mid-1951, this had become standard operating procedures. A 72-acre United Nations Military Cemetery had been opened in Tanggok, Korea along with the Eighth Army's Central Identification Laboratory. During the last two years of the conflict, refrigerated railroad cars transported remains from forward collecting points to

Tannggok. A pattern developed that had the bodies of U.S. Korean War dead recovered and returned to the USA within 30 days time.

The Vietnam War is America's longest conflict and the proficiency of the Army's GRREG units improved considerably compared to all prior wars. This war had less unaccounted for dead. Helicopters allowed the remains to be evacuated from the battlefield in minutes rather than in many hours or days. Combat units themselves became responsible for the initial recovery. Two well-equipped mortuaries were established in Vietnam, one in Da Nang in the north and one in Tan Son Nhut near Saigon in the south. Positive identification was made in these facilities using new laboratory methods along with fingerprint and dental comparisons.

By the end of the war in Indochina, only 28 bodies of fallen American soldiers remained unidentified. By 1984, the remains of one serviceman continued to be classified as unidentified. On Memorial Day of that year were interned at the "Tomb of the Unknown" at Arlington National Cemetery. Fourteen years later, in 1998, the identification process had become so accurate and sophisticated that positive identification of this Vietnam War unknown soldier was made through DNA testing and the now identified Air Force pilot's remains were returned to his home town for reburial.

The mission of the mortuary affairs soldiers in today's U.S. Army has changed little since Captain James M. Moore's men achieved a perfect 100 percent identification rate during the Civil War. Only the name of the job has changed recently along with evacuation and identification techniques that make identification a virtually one hundred percent certainty. The current level of sophistication utilized to identify future KIAs (killed in action) all but insures that the "Tomb of the Unknown" has received its last occupant.

The three dozen or so men and women soldiers who made up the GRREG team that was deployed to Guyana on November 20, 1978, was composed of enlisted soldiers who held the military occupational specialty, 92M. At that time, they were called Graves Registration Specialists, but they are now known as Mortuary Affairs Specialists. Quartermaster officers with the added skill identifier of 4V lead these enlisted personnel.

When they were sent to Jonestown, the GRREG soldiers were operating according to procedures found in U.S. Army Field manual 10-63-1, entitled: Graves Registration Handbook. This now obsolete publication was last issued in July of 1986. The Joint Humanitarian Task Force to Guyana was the largest recovery operation ever performed by U.S. Army GRREG troops. A few years prior to this, the remains of around 330 civilians who perished in a horrible airplane crash at Teneriffe in the Canary Islands were collected, processed and evacuated by some of these same 92Ms. Jonestown represented a challenge nearly three times larger than the one faced in the Canary Islands.

From 1988 to 1991, talented actor Michael Boatman, played Graves Registration Specialist Samuel Beckett on ABC's celebrated television series "China Beach." The show was about the lives of servicemen and women working in a field hospital near Da Nang during the Vietnam War. The character Samuel Beckett was the first graves registration specialist to be depicted in a television series. Boatman created and portrayed this recurring supporting actor role of Beckett as an extremely sensitive, highly educated, articulate and serious man.

The humanitarian mission to Jonestown was the only time I ever had the opportunity to associate with graves registration personnel and to observe them in the performance of their duties. They were not like Beckett. Jonestown was a mass-death scene of unduplicated proportion. The events that occurred there happened in an extremely hot tropical climate that caused all sorts of complications and created the potential for many serious problems that had to be overcome. The heat hastened the decomposition process of the 914 bodies and served as a very real health hazard to the GRREG team. Their daily activities in Guyana were strenuous and strength-sapping. The mental strain is almost beyond comprehension.

It is a tribute to the leadership skills of the noncommissioned officers who led the various participants in the task force and the physical condtioning of those soldiers assigned to that repugnant assignment of identifying and retrieving the 914 victims of the Jonestown slaughter/suicide that only one experienced an injury. Their highly honed physical and mental conditioning permitted them to complete the mission under the worst possible conditions. Undoubtedly, for the members of the force that were not graves registration specialists, there are lasting scars of a psychological nature that will never heal.

I cannot comment on the psychological health of the members of the GRREG team, other than to say, it must take very special people to perform the tasks their occupation requires, without it having some sort of detrimental affect on their psyches. The sick senses of humor exhibited by some of them would shock most people. However, when one's work involves recovering and evacuating the mortal remains of one's own species after those remains have been subjected to the horrific traumas of war or catastrophe, no doubt one's attitudes and sensibilities are different from those of people with so-called normal vocations.

That is my way of stating, as neutrally and nonjudgementally as possible, that some of the activities and interactions I observed and experienced with members of the GRREG team seemed bizarre bordering on psychotic. Most military operations often produce isolated, weird side-shows. The macabre and grotesque nature of this mission simply provided more opportunities to react to the weirdness already in place.

Don't get me wrong, they were extremely professional in the accomplishment of their duties, performing the most gruesome and sickening tasks required of them with the utmost proficiency and without any complaining whatsoever. The lack of bitching was especially strange, when one considers soldiers in general are often notorious complainers. But the things they said and did in response to questions or apparently to relieve the monumental stress and tension of their job, were quite unnerving.

I don't think I will ever forget the graves registration specialists who had the task of bringing the residents of Jonestown home. America owes a debt of gratitude to the GRREG team members.

> "Let us so live that when we come to die even the undertaker will be sorry."
>
> **Mark Twain**

Seven

Innocent Detachment

The lengthening shadows of the tall trees on the western edge of the clearing that the People's Temple members cut out of the thick Guyanan jungle to create Jonestown indicated that my first day in this place of death would soon be drawing to a close. I was nearing the end of my tour of the commune with Lieutenant Abbott of the GDF when the first of the huge U.S. Air Force Jolly Green Giant helicopters were landing on the soccer field to deposit their passengers and cargo. The clouds had dissipated and the sun had sunk below the tree line, but the daylight was not noticeably diminished at that time of the afternoon.

It was obvious that the residents of this American enclave, literally carved out of the South American jungle, were denied the opportunity to see a sunrise or sunset as long as they began and ended their days in Jonestown. The tall trees blocked any semblance of what could be considered a horizon and the sun was high in the sky before its rays reached the cleared area where the village sat. Sunset came every day long after the shadows of the trees completely covered the ground and long before the daylight left the rest of the region.

As the members of the GRREG team collected their personal gear and equipment from the still running helicopters and deposited it at a central point along the edge of the soccer field, the six tough and extremely professional U.S. Special Forces soldiers who had accompanied them were surveying the site. They were looking for vehicles and other pieces of machinery that would facilitate the jobs of the men and women who would be spending the next eight days recovering and evacuating the remains of 914 dead Americans to the United States Air Force Base in Dover, Delaware easier.

By now, I had completed the shocking tour of Jonestown and was discussing the distribution of malaria prophylactic medication with the Special Forces medic who would be remaining in Jonestown with his team to provide security for and assist the GRREG team. Since generators, fuel and light sets had been brought in on the now departed helicopters, no one was worried about the impending darkness that was quickly enveloping Jonestown. Three of the Green Beret troops were in the process of readying the generators to light up the night. Someone wondered out loud if this would help dissuade the ghosts of the recently dead residents from haunting them this first night they were to spend as uninvited guests in their town.

The commune had become eerily quiet. The GRREG soldiers were continuing their meeting with their platoon leader. The Guyanan Defense Force Detachment soldiers were far enough away from our location that their voices were inaudible, even though some seemed to be engaged in animated conversations. As my medic friend and I finished up our business, we observed the scene around us. While the surrounding jungle was teeming with the sounds of awakening wildlife, mostly birds and small creatures of the night, the entire environment was otherwise entirely devoid of any human-made sounds.

Suddenly, without warning... a snap! It was somewhat reminiscent of a rifle being shot and it came from the large barnlike building nearby. Before any of us had the opportunity to hit the dirt, as was our immediate inclination, the sound of the Jonestown generator could be heard as it started up and the outside lights of the commune became illuminated.

"Photoelectric cell," murmured one of the Green Berets to no one in particular. Our generator set was puny and unneeded after discovery of the sophisticated and powerful system already operating in Jonestown.

The GRREG soldiers and the Green Berets soon settled in for the night, setting up their living area upwind from the mass of bodies near the Pavilion. By November 20, the smell was almost unbearably sickening to the uninitiated. My Green Beret friends from Fort Gulick, Panama appeared to be coping well despite their unfamiliarity with the awful stench of death. None of the GRREG personnel were heard to complain about the odor. It was almost as if it was expected as something that came with the job. No matter how ugly or difficult things got, these amazing soldiers whose main mission in the military was to serve the dead, took things in stride. They seemed silently proud of the fact that they were unaffected by sights and smells that made other less-prepared soldiers physically ill.

It was interesting to observe different members of the GRREG team from afar. I was impressed by the professionalism with which they approached even the most sickening and horrifying tasks. Never complaining, never exhibiting signs of disgust, never showing the slightest hint that the task of bagging and processing 914 dead Americans (including hundreds of infants and children) was one they would rather not perform, they maintained their military bearing throughout the mission.

The attitude that was displayed by all of the GRREG personnel, from the oldest veteran to the newest and least experienced members of the team, can only be described as an intense detachment. The reality of the situation was that 914 American citizens had recently been killed and/or voluntarily committed suicide. Their mortal remains lay decomposing in the hot smoldering tropical climate of Guyana, the fluids and chemicals inside them cooking and combining to create gases that were the most noxious I had ever encountered. For most people, this assault on the senses would cause them to wretch, vomit uncontrollably and possibly even faint. The average citizen could suffer many months of nightmares and their personal relationships with loved ones could possibly be negatively impacted on.

Although I have been unable to confirm it, at least one account written by Charles Huff, (one of the Special Forces soldiers on the mission to Jonestown) reported that 16 American servicemen who participated in the Joint Humanitarian Task Force to Guyana committed suicide within a year after their return from that country.

The U.S. Army GRREG soldiers appeared not to consider the human implications of what had occurred. They approached the carnage at Jonestown as just another day at the office. Oh, it was a stressful day no doubt, not like any other day they had ever experienced before, but one which would challenge their capabilities and cause them to find new and creative ways to accomplish their gruesome mission. These men and women appeared to love their job and genuinely seemed to be happy to be in Jonestown, the only place on earth at the time that had a huge amount of work for them to perform.

One GRREG soldier told me as we talked at the end of the mission, "This job is like any other job in the Army. You do it right, you feel the pride of a job well done." Still, their detachment seemed very bizarre to most of us nonGRREG soldiers. Perhaps our actions and comments seemed odd to them.

On November 21, just as the GRREG team was preparing to begin bagging the remains of the fallen People's Temple members in Jonestown, an American television news crew arrived at the commune. Since the GDF was supposed to be blocking the media from entering the site on this the first day of the mission, no one was quite sure how these journalists had gotten in; or what should be done now that they were there. A Public Affairs Lieutenant Colonel from the 193rd Infantry Brigade was on the ground in Jonestown at the time and he was asked by Colonel Gordon, the Joint Task Force Commander, to liaison with the news crew.

The reporter asked if it would be alright to conduct a short interview with one of the female GRREG soldiers he saw preparing to recover the remains laying all around. Two women soldiers were present on the team, one a black Guyanese who was serving in the United

States Army and the other, a caucasian blonde-haired blue-eyed young 19-year-old from South Carolina. Both of these soldiers appeared excited about the mission but, not to the point that they were nervous. It was more like the excitement displayed by a lawyer who is trying his first case or a police officer who is issuing his first speeding ticket.

The veteran news reporter chose the young blonde as his interviewee. She obviously needed no calming down, but nevertheless, the reporter briefly told her to relax and not to be nervous. He told her the tenor of the questions he would be asking and instructed her to simply look into the camera and answer his questions in a clear and normal voice. In no way did this young female soldier appear nervous. In fact, she seemed excited about being on television and said she hoped her folks back home in Columbia would be watching that network's news the night the story appeared.

The Public Affairs Officer reminded the girl that she represented the U.S. Army and he said he knew she would do so with dignity and professionalism. The cute blonde assured him that she would. The Lieutenant

Colonel must have had visions of American teenage boys enlisting in the U.S. Army after seeing this fresh and attractive young American woman on the news, for he stood back with his arms folded across his massive chest and a broad smile on his face. Obviously he felt he had made the right decision as the female graves registration specialist was positioned for the interview.

An area was chosen where her fellow team members could be observed in the background, unloading and separating bundles of body bags and generally preparing to perform the task of readying the remains for transport out of the jungle to the airport in Georgetown. From there, they would be loaded into aluminum coffins before being placed on C140 transport aircraft for the trip to Dover, Delaware. Her comrades all seemed oblivious to the interview that was about to be conducted, just as the reporter had instructed.

After checking his microphone and insuring the big aluminum reflectors were properly held by the news crew members, the reporter began his interview. He managed to get the young blonde soldier to identify herself and tell what her job was. Everything was going along well. The reporter and his crew seemed confident they were getting the story they wanted. The Lieutenant Colonel Public Affairs Officer seemed pleased that the young soldier, so inexperienced in dealing with the press was doing so well. The soldier herself seemed to be the most relaxed person in Jonestown that morning.

As the young female soldier stood confidently waiting for the reporter's next question, he said, "I imagine this is a pretty traumatic experience for you, a 19-year-old girl from Columbia, South Carolina; to have to come down here to Guyana to bring the bodies of all these dead American citizens back home."

"Oh no sir, I'm really looking forward to it," said the bubbly private-first-class beaming brightly, "I wasn't in the Army in time to go to the Canary Island Disaster so this is the first chance I've had to work with real bodies. I'm really looking forward to it," she concluded exuberantly.

A look of horror overcame the Public Affairs Officer who saw his entire military career and chance of making bird colonel flash before his eyes. The reporter stared at the excited young lady, unprepared for her response and unable to formulate an appropriate follow up question. Colonel Gordon simply watched the scene quietly and without expression. I feel that deep down inside he understood her enthusiasm and in a way was proud of that young soldier. Later, he asked the news reporter if he was going to use that one the news. "No way," was the savvy reporter's two word reply.

That evening on his network's news broadcast, the reporter was shown dong a stand-up that was accompanied by footage of the dead residents of Jonestown waiting to be taken away and the living GRREG soldiers preparing to do just that. The young blonde's parents never saw their daughters moment of glory. The GRREG soldiers who went on working behind the interview never indicated they thought her response was less than normal.

The response of this young GRREG soldier was shocking to those who viewed and heard it who were not trained to process human remains. It seemed normal to those whose job it was to care for the dead.

Dispassionate detachment is a requirement for men and women whose jobs call for them to handle bodies that are subjected to the massive damage created by war or catastrophe. Along with the attribute of dispassionate indifference, this attractive young lady seemed to have a genuine and refreshing innocence. With the passage of nearly twenty years since the event occurred, one might wonder if she has maintained her detachment? Has she made a career of the military? How does she view her role at Jonestown? Was she able to maintain her detachment and innocence? It seems she would have to if she were to maintain her sanity while performing the job of caring for those who have been killed under less than sane circumstances.

The GRREG team advance party and the six Green Beret troops spent a restless Monday night in Jonestown. While the Special Forces soldiers from Panama were familiar with the strange exotic sounds that emanated from the jungle throughout the night, the troops sent down to Guyana from the United States to collect the dead of Jonestown were not. Animals and birds of the night, signalling each other in the darkness, became forboding and unknown creatures the soldiers knew nothing about. Fear of the unknown is the worst fear of all.

At this early stage of the Joint Task Force's humanitarian mission, it was felt that many of the residents of this enclave of Americans, far from home, had taken to the jungles surrounding Jonestown to avoid participating in the People's Temple final deadly ritual. The ever-alert Green Berets were keeping a close watch on the fringes of the clearing in which the commune was built and along the encompassing tree line. They were looking for any survivors that may find their way back to Jonestown. The sounds the Special Forces soldiers were hoping to hear from the jungle were not the normal noises of the insects, animals and birds, but the alien human cries for help from anyone who survived the evilness that had consumed close to 1,000 of their family and friends.

Although they never heard a human voice coming from the jungle that night, the Green Berets were not troubled, for what they heard was expected. The human noises they so hoped to hear were absent because the handful of residents that did escape the slaughter of Saturday night had all made it to safety by Sunday morning. Some had walked the railroad tracks to Matthews Ridge 14 miles to the south. A smaller number, including Odell Rhodes, took their individual chances by walking along the dirt road that led to Port Kaitumba, five miles from the carnage.

The noises of the jungle bothered most of the GRREG team. Unaccustomed to hearing the strange calls of the jungle they spent much of the night opining and arguing about what animals were making what sounds and how dangerous they were. The young troopers discussed the macabre and unbelievable scene of horror and death. The dead residents of Jonestown were no cause of fear for the GRREG troops. While a few of them had little or no hands-on experience processing actual cadavers, all believed that once they became lifeless, the residents of Jonestown lost the ability to feel or inflict pain. These were not a superstitious group of young American soldiers. They did not fear ghosts or spirits, for they shared the belief that death is a final and finite end to existence for the mortal body, formerly inhabited by a living being. They had seen and heard about the natural and unnatural results and consequences of death but had never experienced the supernatural.

The six Special Forces men who shared the experience of Jonestown that night, with the GRREG troops, did have a reason to fear the dead of Jonestown though. Terrorists or anyone else bent on causing harm to those living in the commune that night could very easily use the dead to infiltrate into the very areas the living of Jonestown were now occupying. With so many bodies laying in every direction from where the American troops were bivuacked, all a dedicated terrorist would need to do would be to advance ever so slowly among the corpses, stopping and laying stone still on top of or beside them as the terrorist inched his way ever so slowly toward any living being he wished to harm. So while the Green Beret soldiers didn't actually fear the nearly 1000 dead of Jonestown who surrounded them, they remained wary of any movement of living humans who might try to use the dead to help him wreak havoc on the American troops.

Rumors already had been circulating that the cult had "hit squads" that had taken to the jungle in search of last minute defectors who were unwilling to participate in the final sacred ritual ordered by Rev. Jones. By this point in the operation, the U.S. Embassy was well aware of the contact that Jones had with the Soviet Embassy during his nearly two years in Guyana. It was also common knowledge that the Cubans provided a great deal of technical support to the Marxist Guyanan government.

The GRREG troops feared the animals and the Green Berets feared the dead who could be used as a bizarre form of concealment. To the former, the dead represented normalcy and the animals represented danger. To the latter, it was the dead that posed a threat and the jungle creatures who created a bit of normalcy in a world gone mad for the present moment.

The deep darkness of the night was replaced by the first gray shadows of dawn as the sun rose in the eastern sky. The sounds of three U.S. Army UH1 helicopters could barely be heard coming from the same direction as the sun. Working all night long at Timheri Airport, soldiers from the 193rd Infantry Brigade meticulously and efficiently reassembled the three helicopters transported from Panama as cargo inside U.S. Air Force C130's. By 0330 hours on Tuesday, November 21, the crews of the choppers were going through their pre-flight checks in preparation for their 150 mile flight to Jonestown.

At the same time, more soldiers from the GRREG team sent from Fort Lee, Virginia were waking up and packing their personal gear so they could ride the UH1s into Jonestown. Colonel William Gordon, the Joint Task Force commander was also getting ready to join the advance party along with his small staff from the United States Army Southern Command in Panama.

The three olive drab helicopters that had taken off from the Timheri Airport in Georgetown, allowing for an ETA (estimated time of arrival) in Jonestown to coincide with the first light of day. And now, early in the morning of November 21, the American troops who were already on the ground arose from their abbreviated rest. Laying under poncho liners that protected them from the heavy dew, they were slowly acclimating their senses to place and time. They heard the familiar sound of the Army choppers approaching and they knew the first of many more demanding days to come was about to commence.

With the arrival of the rest of the GRREG troops, would come the first day of the actual recovery of human remains that littered Jonestown. Nine hundred and fourteen people who had lost their lives three days before, but who were still a long way from any final resting place, would be the object of an intense effort of identification and evacuation. The identification process had began Sunday, before American troops had arrived in Guyana.

Odell Rhodes and a few other Jonestown residents who were resourceful or fortunate enough to be spared, returned to this place of horror on Sunday to assist the GDF and Guyanese government officials in the identification process of the already badly bloated bodies. They did the best they could, often only being able to offer the nickname or first name of their former friends. The names were then scrawled onto pieces of cardboard that were attached to the bodies. This effort by people who must have been in shock and scared to death was admirable, but it was too little too late. If the deceased had not already fashioned his or her own bracelet and placed it on the wrist before he or she died, chances are identification would not occur for many days or weeks at Dover Air Force Base.

As soon as the helicopters landed in the soccer field and dropped off the GRREG personnel, they became airborne again. Soon the jungles around Jonestown reverberated with the sounds of American choppers flying search patterns, using loud speaker systems to urge any survivors who had fled to the jungle to make their way to the now safe Jonestown.

For three hours these three birds of modern warfare hovered, searched and pleaded for survivors to come out of the dense jungles. The only time they landed during that three hour period was to refuel at Matthews Ridge Air Field. It turned out to be a frustrating exercise in futility. The jungle was not going to reveal even one survivor of the carnage at Jonestown. The dozen or so who had managed to live through this nightmare had been discovered by the GDF or Guyanan civilians in or near Matthews Ridge or Port Kaitumba many hours before.

It was a confusing and disappointing morning for the American rescuers who were convinced by the over 800 U.S. passports recovered in Jonestown and by a preliminary error-filled body count, that underestimated the actual number by almost 550, that hundreds of American residents of Jonestown had escaped drinking the cyanide poison. Following three hours of appeals from the air without results, the search was called off. The question remained: What were the fates of the unaccounted for residents of Jonestown?

"How fascinating is death, the extinction of life. One moment here and the next gone. The light put out and only the empty bag of the body left." **Unknown**

Eight

"Just wait until they open this one in Dover"

Guyana is located on the northeast shoulder of South America. It covers about 83,000 square miles and is bordered by the countries of Venezuela to the northwest, Brazil on the west and south and by Surinam on the east. Its northern border is the Atlantic Ocean.

All but about 30 percent of Guyana is made up of tropical rain forest. The country is located just north of the equator. It rains 80 to 100 inches a year and the temperatures are usually in the high 80s and 90s during the day.

Guyana is said to be one of the most beautiful countries in South America, with many rivers and waterfalls. But for most of the Americans taking part in this mission, beauty is not what they will remember about Guyana. If the jungle area around Jonestown was rich in exotic wildlife and flora, none of us noticed it because we were too overwhelmed by the ugliness and horrible stench that accompanies mass death. Grossly bloated bodies, deformed by so many hours of exposure to the heat of the tropical sun that they burst and deposited copious amounts of their putrid foul-smelling contents onto the earth, have a way of striking one blind to anything lovely.

As soon as the rest of the GRREG team joined the advance party, they all received a briefing from Colonel Gordon. The preliminary work of trying to identify the remains then commenced. Jonestown was divided into sections and the remains found in each section were catalogued and tagged. The preparation for evacuation was executed in a precise, coordinated manner.

For the newly arrived mortuary affairs specialists who were now fanning out in to all areas of the clearing that made up the commune, the full extent of the carnage was quickly becoming apparent. Many who participated in this unique mission thought the identification process alone would be next to impossible. Comparatively few of the 914 bodies bore the handmade ID bracelets many family members attached to their wrists before taking the poison and even fewer had been identified by Odell Rhodes and his team of Jonestown survivor volunteers.

The condition of the bodies at this point in time, four days after the mass murder/suicide, made further visual identification impossible except for a very few like the Reverend Jim Jones himself who was among the first to be catalogued, tagged and bagged by the GRREG personnel. This was very disconcerting to some of these troops whose lives were dedicated to the business of processing the remains of human beings after catastrophic events and who prided themselves on being able to identify the vast majority of remains at any site of mass death they worked.

In a wartime situation, the ID tags worn by soldiers invariably provide positive proof of identity. In airplane crashes and natural disasters that involve the loss of many lives, wallets and jewelry can often be used to place a name to the victim.

But the remains of the residents of Jonestown posed problems that the GRREG team members had never encountered before in such huge numbers. Very few of the dead carried wallets or wore jewelry. By Tuesday, the bodies were badly bloated with heads resembling those of hydrocephalic children. They were in such an advanced state of decomposition, recognition was not possible. The color of almost every victim was a dark blue-black, making it difficult to determine even the ethnicity of a corpse.

The fact that nearly everyone who perished, be they caucasian or black, now shared the same color was a strange irony because the man they followed to their death, Jim Jones, was recognizably Caucasian. It was as if the members of the People's Temple had finally achieved a form of equality in death and the evil person who led them to their eternal grave did not share this attribute.

There were name tags sewn into most of the clothing worn by the residents of Jonestown. Unfortunately, the communal lifestyle makes for the sharing of wardrobes, so many corpses wore clothes bearing two or three different names, none of which were actually their own.

The task of identifying the bodies was a fouler operation... even more so than the process of placing the remains into the body bags. During the identification process, bodies had to be individually checked, pockets turned inside-out and ID bracelets read and recorded. This meant touching and handling the rapidly decomposing remains, many of which were already displaying the eggs lain by the millions of flies drawn to the scene. Maggots covered the entire area where the bodies lay.

One common form of life usually found wherever death in the tropics occurs was conspicuously missing from the skies over Jonestown. One can only speculate about the absence of buzzards. These scavenger birds are as common in the warmer climes as cardinals are in Missouri. Perhaps these birds that feed off carrion and keep the environment clean, realized the men, women and children of Jonestown died from the ingestion of a deadly poison. We may never know what caused the buzzards to stay away, but for me, as an old tropical hand and a long time resident of South Texas where the birds are common, their absence in Jonestown added to the unrealness of the occasion.

The first attempts to pick up the bodies by grasping their heads and limbs and lifting them into the bags, more often than not, caused a limb or two or a head to become detached from its bloated liquid-filled torso. When this happened, a foul thick serous fluid would stream from the body part being held by a hapless soldier and an even larger amount would flow from the torso as it landed back down on the ground. Because the bodies were in such close proximity to one another, it wasn't long before the soil in Jonestown became a muddy mix of dirt and smelly human borne liquid.

As the first bodies were being bagged, I was sitting in our aid station in Matthews Ridge, breathing the air that was not fouled by the bodies in Jonestown. Fourteen miles is a long way for an odor to travel and being south of the commune, in an area where the prevailing winds flow east and west, we had little to fear that our atmosphere would become contaminated like that of Jonestown.

I knew the process occurring in Jonestown that morning involved the bodies being tagged and bagged where they lay, then they were loaded onto a trailer towed by the commune's tractor and driven to the edge of the landing zone adjoining the soccer field. The body bags would be placed directly on the Jolly Green Giants from the trailer and then flown 150 miles to Timheri Airport in Georgetown, where they would be placed in aluminum coffins that were marked with the occupant's identity, if it was known.

Every hour, the U.S. Army communications man in Jonestown would radio his body count report for us to relay to Georgetown. During the first hour after the operation to evacuate the bodies began, less than 10 of the dead had been bagged. An similar count was called in after the second hour. Then, before it was time for the next hourly radio transmission, we received a rather odd request from Jonestown.

"Tell HQ we need snow shovels." was the curt statement that came across the airwaves. Snow shovels? Guyana is a tropical country that has never seen snow. How would we be able to procure snow shovels for Jonestown and why did they need them?

The call for the unusual cold weather implements was dutifully relayed to the Task Force Headquarters at

Timheri Airport and from there to the U.S. Air Force Base at Charleston, South Carolina. Within six hours, three dozen snow shovels arrived in Jonestown for use by the GRREG personnel.

With the arrival of these simple tools so alien to this region of the world, the process of placing the rotting remains in body bags was streamlined considerably. Usually, six or eight soldiers, three or four on each side of the very fragile body, would lift it in unison, a foot or so off the ground. Two other soldiers would then slide an open body bag under the suspended snow shovels and the remains would be gently deposited inside.

This procedure sounds simple, but it wasn't always as successful as the GRREG team members hoped it would be. The body juices continued to flow freely from orifices and breaks in the skin, creating a slippery, gooey mess. Sometimes a heavy head, two times its normal size, would slip from the shovel and fall to the earth below with a thud after it became severed from the fragile neck.

For the most part, the bagging process was made much more efficient by the novel and unconventional use of the snow shovels. A definite increase in the GRREG team's productivity was noted when the hourly reports were relayed. We maintained a running cumulative total of the bodies bagged. By the end of the first day, nearly 100 bodies had been evacuated from Jonestown to Timheri Airport.

Wednesday found more than three times that number had been processed with the cumulative total reaching over 400. Those of us in Matthews Ridge, away from the actual gruesome scene being played out in Jonestown, found that figure curious because initially it had been reported by the GDF that around 400 Americans had perished on November 18. Now, here it was five days later and the body count continued to mount.

But in Jonestown, there was no mystery. After evacuating the remains of nearly 450 adult Americans who died in the massacre, it had become obvious the bulk of the residents had lain themselves atop one another, in layers if you will, after ingesting the cyanide-laced Fla-Vor-Ade.

When the audio tape of Jones urging his flock to participate in the ritual suicide is studied and one is able to view the topography of the land, it appears the infants and babies who had the poison forced down their tiny throats by their mothers using needle-less syringes, were placed at the bottom of a large somewhat concave area near the pavilion. The toddlers represented the second wave of surely uncooperative victims to be killed and they were placed on top of the babies. Next came the pre-adolescents, then the adolescents, then the young teens, all taking their last drinks on earth in turn, or having the poison forced upon them, then taking their places on top of younger siblings who preceded them. The fiendish ritual delivered a horrific death.

The senior citizens of Jonestown were the next to go, along with some of the mothers who were grieving because of the remorse they felt at having murdered their own children moments before. These people, young and old, all became part of the pile that appeared flat because of the lay of the land. Finally, able-bodied adult residents of the commune, either voluntarily or by force, drank the cyanide-filled fruit drink and became the final layer of what looked like 400 victims, but was actually an inverted pyramid of more than twice that number of dead.

Thursday November 23, 1978 was Thanksgiving Day, perhaps the most miserable one ever spent by the 100 or so American troops who had journeyed to

Jonestown to retrieve the remains of their countrymen who died there. By now, the evacuation process had become old hat and harmless diversions were practiced by the GRREG personnel to make their hard tedious work under the hot sun seem to go by faster. One team of baggers would race another to see how many bags each could manage to fill in an hour. Maybe it helped some of the soldiers to cope with the sickening scene they were plunged into, but there came a flow of sick grape Kool-Ade jokes. They were anything but politically correct and they forever falsely stigmatizing the beverage as the drink of choice at the Jonestown Massacre. One graves registration specialist with a musical inclination composed a song about Jonestown in his precious spare time. It never made the Top 40 charts.

But even the jokes, contests and songs could not take the minds of the American troops off of the football games and related parades they were missing. So too they missed Mom's home style turkey dinners; or even the holiday feast mess halls in Panama and the States were serving on this day. The troops in Jonestown did enjoy their first hot meal since arriving in Guyana on this day, however, in the form of Swanson's Roast Turkey TV Dinners that had been heated up at Timheri Airport and flown in by helicopter.

By Friday, November 24, the routine in Jonestown continued and the body count had increased to nearly 650. An absence of body bags brought the mission to a halt... at least temporarily. More were quickly flown in from the United States. Most of the adult victims of the massacre had been removed from Jonestown by this day and even the GRREG troops were horrified to find most of the remains that were left were those of pre-teens and babies. A total of 270 children had been murdered in Jonestown on November 18, 1978. The sad truth is that most of the young victims of the Jonestown Massacre were never identified and occupy a mass grave in California.

Since body bags were in short supply and since the remains of the children were unidentifiable, the ingenious GRREG personnel decided they would put the bodies of two or more children into one body bag. By this time, the job was becoming an exhausting one and even the most rabid of mortuary specialists were ready to clean up and go home.

"Wait until they open this one in Dover"

On Sunday, November 26, by the time the last Jolly Green Giant helicopter of the day lifted from the Jonestown soccer field, all but about 50 of the massacre victims had been airlifted out. The next time these big choppers would take off from Jonestown, body number 914 would have departed as the last American People's Temple member to leave the commune.

Monday, November 27 marked our last day in Guyana and the official end of the mission that brought 200 American soldiers to this tropical country. I was standing on the hot tarmac at Timheri Airport, thinking of how this country that I had never heard of before would be remembered by most of my generation as the place where the Jonestown Massacre happened.

I was watching as the last helicopter that left Jonestown with bodies touched down. I observed as a group of extremely tired and thoroughly stressed out young American soldiers who had already spent the last seven days of their lives removing the remains of nearly 900 dead Americans from helicopters removed some more for the final time.

As I noted the robot-like movements of these men as they repeated the process of picking a body bag up from the helicopter, walking to the tailgate of a waiting truck and depositing their human cargo onto the truck, I saw that their faces were mask-like, completely devoid of any emotion. Their Army uniforms were soaked beyond cleaning with the sweat of their own skin and fluids from the bodies of the dead they had been salvaging for proper burial back home.

As I gazed upon this depressing scene, Colonel Gordon, the gruff, no-nonsense Joint Task Force commander approached me. "Brailey," he barked, "Did y'all bring any psyche techs (psychiatric technician) with you from Panama?"

"No sir," I answered, "Why?"

"They were tryin' to put that dead go-rilla into a body bag," said Gordon.

Jim Jones had a huge chimpanzee that was kept in a cage near his cottage. Jones called it "Mr. Muggs." It is rumored that small children were put into the cage with the old chimp as a form of punishment.

During my first tour of Jonestown the week before, I saw poor Mr. Muggs. He had been shot to death. That dead chimpanzee smelled much worse than any of the human remains did.

Gordon went on, "They kept tryin' to push that big go-rilla's shoulders into the body bag, but they just couldn't get it to zip up. I watched 'em for a few minutes until one of them graves registration guys was gonna hack its shoulders off with a machete."

"'Hold it!' I commanded," said Colonel Gordon in his loud voice, "Why are you gonna hack that go-rilla up?"

"Because he won't fit into the body bag, sir," was the respectful reply of the ringleader of the GRREG soldiers.

"Why are you puttin' that go-rilla into the body bag anyway?" asked the tired and confused Joint Task Force commander.

"Why, sir? WHY? Just wait until they open this one up in Dover!" was the devilish reply of the leering GRREG soldier.

Gordon told me he said to the practical joker, "Now look son, I don't mind you playin' a joke on them folks up in Dover, but I won't allow you to mutilate that poor go-rilla just to fit him into the bag."

He took the machete away from the soldier and stood back watching. This group of six graves registration specialists who had just spent more than a week bagging the remains of 914 American human beings worked for more than 30 minutes trying to maneuver the dead chimpanzee into the body bag. As the last Jolly Green Giant lifted off from the soccer field with the last sets of human remains from the massacre on November 18, the tireless GRREG troopers were still working hard to pull off their macabre joke.

Like most of the 914 Americans returning home to the United States through the Air Force Base at Dover, Delaware, Mr. Muggs had come to Jonestown from San Francisco. Unlike them, he never returned to the United States.

> "The workings of the human heart are the profoundest mystery of the universe. One moment they make us despair of our kind, and the next we see in them the reflection of the divine image."
>
> Charles W. Chestnutt

Nine

"He has a heat rash"

Matthews Ridge is a formerly bustling town built near the now depleted bauxite mines in northeastern Guyana. During its heyday, some five years before the arrival of the Jonestown Agricultural Commune built by the People's Temple in 1976, Matthews Ridge boasted a population of over 1000 miners and their families. By the time the American residents of Jonestown were victims of their leader's call for ritual suicide/murder, the town had shrunk to around 250, mostly Amerindian residents.

The main industry of the former mining town had become subsistence farming by 1978 and the farmers and their families were barely subsisting. One sure sign that an area is poor is the total lack of refuse found along the roadways. Every bit of waste in Matthews Ridge was recycled, not because of any great concern for the environment, but out of necessity. Discarded empty tin cans become patches for leaky roofs and walls. Waste paper was used to start fires in stoves so the wives and mothers of Matthews Ridge could cook the meager daily meals for their husbands and children.

Our aid station was at the airfield some three miles south of the small town. The only residents at that location were a garrison of 20 or so Guyana Defense Force soldiers who occupied and worked in three buildings on a small mesa overlooking the black tarmac landing strip. We shared a small corner of this flat hill with the GDF troopers.

There was one small building on the edge of the airfield. It was little more than a shack with a large overhanging roof used to shelter travelers from the weather, be it the incessant heat of the sun or the frequent rains that fall during the two four-month rainy seasons. Our U.S. Army aviation fuel specialists had their operation set up at this building.

Two signs adorned the small shack at the airfield. One announced the name of the town to any transients who were not sure of where they were. The other told travelers to the region that they had entered a "Malaria" area and they were required to check in with the local Malaria Control Office.

During our nine days at the airfield, my men and I interacted daily with the GDF soldiers billeted there and with the local folks of Matthews Ridge. Since our daily fare of cold c-rations became boring after only a few days, I managed to trade some of these military-issued meals for some locally produced cheese. The cheese, on some freshly baked Matthews Ridge bread, represented a tasty, albeit still cold change to our diet.

But something happened on Thanksgiving Day that made our already cordial relationship with the GDF soldiers and local population even more friendly. By 1800 hours, the eight Americans manning our outpost at the airfield began to realize that our promised hot Thanksgiving meal was not going to materialize. The thought of eating our all-too-familiar beans and franks instead of traditional turkey and dressing, was depressing to say the least.

Our Air Force communications sergeant radioed the Task Force Headquarters at Timheri Airport to inquire about the eagerly anticipated promised first hot meal in Guyana that had yet to appear on our table. The duty officer at HQ said he would look into the matter and some thirty minutes later informed us that apparently there had been a SNAFU in the delivery of our Thanksgiving meal. But, he guaranteed the situation would be remedied the next day when Thanksgiving dinner with "all the trimmings" would be delivered to our location. He then asked how many Americans were at our site. We responded with the correct number of "eight."

The next morning, at approximately 0900 hours, the first helicopter from Georgetown arrived at the Matthews Ridge airfield. Samuels and Sanders, two well known connoisseurs of fine food, galloped to the just arriving chopper. As the crew chief slid the door open, Samuels looked inside and quickly motioned for some help. All the Americans at the outpost except for the Air Force communications man on radio watch ran down to assist in removing our belated holiday meal from the helicopter.

Our special dinner was packed in five large boxes. After bringing them back to our tent, Sanders opened the first one. It contained 40 Swanson's Roast Turkey TV dinners, still in the individual packaging, but fully cooked, heated and still warm. Another box contained an equal number of the dinners. Two other boxes contained 160 half-pints of milk packed in dry ice. The last box held fresh fruits and canisters of mixed nuts, enough food to satisfy 80 hungry servicemen, not eight!

While Sanders and Samuels wanted to dig in right away and see what kind of dent our team could make in these rations meant for ten times more people than were present, saner thoughts ruled as Fields suggested we invite the local GDF garrison and some of the local young people, mostly females of course, to partake in our Thanksgiving feast. Some of the kids that were already hanging around were told to go get their friends. I walked over to the GDF outpost and invited Sergeant Harper and his comrades to our dinner.

So, on November 24, 1978, a day after the football games were played and most Americans were finished digesting their Thanksgiving feasts of the day before, eight American servicemen far from home taught two dozen Guyanese soldiers and twice that many local teenaged girls about the history of one of their country's most popular holidays. Like the participants in that first Thanksgiving celebration in Massachusetts more than three hundred years before, we invited the locals of Matthews Ridge to share our bounty.

This gesture, which in reality was basically a way to keep good food from being wasted, solidified the friendships we had already began to form with the soldiers and young people of Matthews Ridge five days before. What had begun purely by serendipity with John Wayne Bars on Monday, was cemented on Friday by Specialist Fourth Class Rick Fields, who, I've got to believe, did so with some degree of calculation. He had become very friendly with not just a few of the black teenaged Guyanan girls of Matthews Ridge, all of who enjoyed their first American Thanksgiving meal with us.

Although they had very little of value to share with us, the people of Matthews Ridge gave us more than they know. They were among the kindest and most generous folks I had ever met. From the man who walked three miles from the town to the airfield with me on that dark night, to the friends Sanders and Fields made, to Pauline's grandfather and mother, everyone we came in contact with represented the finest in humankind.

One night, while sitting in Mrs. Pool's bar drinking a beer, a young man came in and sat next to me. He pulled 20 Polaroid photos from his jacket pocket and placed them on the bar in front of me. He told me the photos had been shot at a party in Jonestown, just two weeks before. Reverend Jim Jones would occasionally host parties for the local folks. At this particular event, some prominent Guyanan politicians were also in attendance.

Some photos showed Jones and these politicos. Others showed the American residents of the commune interacting with the local Guyanese. The Jonestown band was depicted in a couple of shots playing music for the guests. All of the pictures showed seemingly content Americans enjoying their roles as hosts to the locals. These pictures made me wonder out loud what could have caused these obviously carefree Americans to participate in the recent mass murder/suicide that snuffed out so many lives.

After studying and discussing each of the instant photos with my new friend, I stacked the lot of them and handed them back to him.

"No," he said, sliding the stack back in front of me, "They are for you, a gift."

"Oh no," I replied, realizing the importance of the photos, "I couldn't possibly take them."

"Please," he replied, "I want you to have them."

Not wishing to offend this kind young man, I told him I would take the photos only if he would allow me to pay for them. In the United States, Polaroid film was and still is quite expensive and I could only imagine how much of a monetary investment these 20 photos represented in Guyana.

Finally, after a few minutes of protest, the young man accepted my offer of ten American dollars for the pictures. After leaving the bar that night and returning back to the airfield, I realized that these photos might be worth money and decided to try to sell them to a news magazine when I returned to Panama. Little did I know at the time, that this innocent purchase would put me in a small amount of jeopardy just a week or so later.

The duty at Matthews Ridge airfield was so routine that boredom was the biggest challenge we had to overcome. The anticipated poison victims had been dead long before we arrived in Guyana. The few first aid problems experienced among the members of the GRREG team in Jonestown were easily handled by the Green Beret medic on the ground there.

Our days were mostly filled with administrative duties. We inventoried supplies and equipment more in those nine days than we ever did in the previous nine months in Panama. I made two short trips to Jonestown, more as a diversion than to accomplish any mission-essential task. We all became competent radio operators by assisting the two Air Force communications men.

My own man, Sanders, actually became the only medical emergency our aid station cared for during the entire nine day stay at Matthews Ridge. His illness occurred on our last day at the airfield.

It was the morning of November 28, the last day the GRREG team would be in Jonestown. The remains of all of the adults and over two-thirds of the children had already been removed from the jungle commune and we had been alerted early that morning that an aircraft would be arriving in the early afternoon to transport us and our equipment to Timheri Airport in Georgetown.

As soon as Samuels, who was on radio watch, informed us of the move out order, we began to break down our supplies and equipment. Specialist Fourth Class Sanders, 20 years old and endowed with more muscle than brains, removed his fatigue jacket and olive drab T-shirt and began to tackle the job of taking our two tentsdown. So intent on going home, he didn't heed my warning to put his shirt back on and slow down.

Within an hour, Sanders was noticeably ill. Perspiring so profusely that his trousers were thoroughly soaked in sweat and appearing pale and weak, I ordered the young medic to sit in the shade of the one tent that was still standing. His skin was cool and clammy and his blood pressure was extremely low.

I also noticed that the front and back of Sanders' exposed torso and arms were covered with red papular lesions. He was obviously suffering from heat exhaustion complicated by *miliaria rubra*, or what is commonly called "prickly heat" or "heat rash."

Either problem alone can be easily managed. While heat exhaustion is a debilitating medical problem, when properly treated with rest and oral fluids, it is quickly reversed. However, when complicated by *miliaria,* which prohibits the sweat glands from functioning to properly cool the body, the combination of conditions constitute a possibly life-threatening medical emergency.

I instructed Rick Fields to begin cooling Sanders with tepid sponge baths and to offer him as much cool water as he could drink. I told Ben Samuels to prepare an intravenous infusion of Normal Saline solution for Sanders while I went over to the radio to consult with our Brigade Surgeon, Major Buenos, at Timheri Airport.

Once we contacted the Joint Task Force Headquarters, the radioman there told us to wait while he sent for a doctor from the medical clearing station that was set up there. After ten minutes that seemed like an eternity, the distant voice of a physician I didn't know came through the speaker on our radio set. While the quality of the voice was understandable, the doctor's speech had a slur to it that made me wonder if he had been imbibing at this early hour of the day.

"Thish ish Doctor Winston, how can I help you?" said the tinny voice. "Say 'Over' sir" came the prompt from the communications man at the airport 150 miles away. "Over" added the physician, unfamiliar with radio protocol.

"Doctor," I said, "I have an otherwise healthy, conscious, 20-year-old Caucasian male with symptoms of severe heat exhaustion complicated by miliaria of the trunk and arms." Worried the radio might cause the doctor to misunderstand what I was saying, I spelled the condition phonetically, "That's miliaria, MIKE -- INDIA -- LIMA -- INDIA -- ALPHA -- ROMEO -- INDIA -- ALPHA, over."

There was a long pause from the Timheri Airport end of the radio call. I decided to continue with my message, "His temperature is normal, pulse is 122, respirations are 32, blood pressure is 92/40. I have began cooling the patient. We are giving him oral fluids and have him lying in the shade with his legs elevated. We are starting an IV of Normal Saline. Do you have any other instructions? Over." The words were presented over the radio in slow distinct segments so the radioman could copy them down.

"What did you say he hash?" queried the Doctor Winston. "Say 'over' sir," coached the radioman. "Over."

"He has heat exhaustion and miliaria. I spell phonetically, MIKE -- INDIA -- LIMA -- INDIA -- ALPHA -- ROMEO -- INDIA -- ALPHA, over," I replied clearly and slowly. The pause repeated.

"I want to evacuate him to your location, over," I went on. "What are your instructions, sir? Over," I said.

After what seemed to be about five minutes, but probably was only a minute or so, Doctor Winston's beery voice boomed over the speaker of our radio. "Have him rest, give him water to drink and start an IV. I want you to bring the patient here, over," he said in a slurred but authoritative voice.

While the Air Force communications sergeant arranged for an air evacuation for Mark, I had a quick meeting with Samuels and Fields. Most of our supplies and equipment had already been packed and palletized. There was nothing left to do but take down one tent and wait for the helicopter that would transport us to Timheri Airfield later in the day. I told my other two comrades that I would accompany Sanders to the clearing station in Georgetown.

Thirty minutes later, an Army U21 arrived to transport us out of Matthew Ridge. While winging our way toward the airport 150 miles away, I noticed the speed of the aircraft was well into the red warning area on the gauge on the control panel. I told the pilot that our emergency wasn't so severe that we had to risk flying faster than is safe and he told me to take care of my patient and he'd take care of flying the plane.

We did arrive safely at Timheri Airport. Medics from the clearing station sent down from Fort Bragg, North Carolina, met us and took Sanders to a waiting field ambulance for transport to the nearby Admissions & Disposition section. I saw Captain Snow and Major Buenos standing in an open doorway at the old terminal so I walked over to give them a report.

As I related the details of Sander's heat injury and the difficult time I had communicating with the clearing station's physician, an obviously soused Army lieutenant colonel physician approached and asked if I was the medic who brought the patient with the heat injury in just now. I stated I was and the arrogant doctor with the obvious drinking problem, looked at me and said derisively, "He doesn't have malaria, he has a heat rash!"

All I could manage to respond was, "Yes, sir. Thank you sir," and the tipsy doctor turned around and stumbled back to his unit.

"He's been like that every day," was the sad explanation Major Buenos had for Doctor Winston's performance.

Ten

The Final Dance With Death

After my astonishing run-in with the inebriated Army doctor, I felt the need for a cold Banks Beer. At this point in my military career I had been a medic for ten years and had never encountered a physician who was noticeably drunk on duty. To the credit of doctors in the Army, I never saw one during the second and final decade of my time in the Army either.

Fortunately, the U.S. State Department had arranged for the entire task force to enjoy some of Guyana's finest brew on this the final day of the mission. It was preparing to throw perhaps the biggest party in the history of after-mission parties. One hundred and forty four cases of Banks Beer were stacked against one wall of the tired old Timheri Airport terminal. Blocks of ice had been chopped and placed on top of and among the cases. Beside the beer were bottles of DM Gold Label Rum, the pride of Guyana's distilling industry. This is the smoothest rum in the world. True connoisseurs of fine rum would never dream of ruining a drink of DM Gold Label with ice or Coca Cola.

Perhaps it was no wonder the clearing platoon doctor was so drunk. It was obvious this country was an alcoholic's paradise. What with a bottle of beer selling for twenty American cents and the rum being so mellow it is practically addictive, the liver of any overly imbibing visitor to Guyana would be in constant overload and in danger of shutting down. And here were 3456 bottles of beer and over 200 fifths of rum waiting to be shared by a couple of hundred tired and stressed out soldiers who didn't need an excuse to party. If everyone were to equally partake in their fair share of this bounty, each member of the force would be drinking 17 beers and a bottle of rum over the next eight to ten hours. Thankfully, the embassy remembered to provide mixed nuts and canned Frito Corn

Chips. Heaven forbid we should do all the drinking on an empty stomach.

I was standing alone in the middle of the fairly empty, abandoned terminal building, drinking a cold Banks and missing the men I had left behind in Matthews Ridge. Major Buenos and Captain Snow had left to attend a meeting. I was a stranger here, having left Georgetown to support the operation at Jonestown before most of the troops currently working here had arrived in country.

As I tried hard not to feel sorry for myself, a jeep entered a wide doorway at the far end of the huge open building. It quickly reached the point where I was standing and the lone occupant, a black American Major, with the last name of "Major," asked me to get him a beer. I ambled over to a wooden case that had a block of ice imbedded into the necks of the 24 bottles of beer that occupied it. I lifted the shrinking block of ice, removed a frosty cold bottle of Banks and replaced the natural refrigerant from whence it came. Using one of the dozens of silver church keys tied to the cases, I popped the metal cap from the brown glass bottle, walked over to the major sitting in the driver's seat of the jeep and handed him the cold brew.

"Haven't seen you around," said the friendly and unpretentious young Quartermaster Corps officer.

"No sir, just got here, I've been forward, I replied.

"Forward? Jonestown?" questioned Major Major.

"Yes sir, Jonestown a few times, mostly in Matthews Ridge," I said.

"Well, I guess dead bodies don't bother you then do they?" the major said in more of a statement than a question.

"No sir, not really, I've seen and smelled enough of them lately," I said flatly.

"Good!" said Major Major enthusiastically. "Want to get your picture in the paper?"

"I guess so," I answered.

"Hop in," said the Quartermaster officer, patting the passenger seat.

I climbed into the jeep and before I had a chance to settle in my seat, Major Major threw the vehicle in reverse, did a quick half turn, jammed the jeep's gear shift into first gear and tooled out of the terminal toward the tarmac. As we raced toward the flight line where trucks and tired soldiers could be seen waiting for the incoming Jolly Green Giant helicopters and the last full body bags from

Jonestown. When the two big incoming metal birds deposited their sad cargo at Timheri Airport, the first part of the Joint Task Force's mission, the recovery and evacuation of the remains of over 900 Americans from Jonestown would be complete.

The soldiers waiting for the final flights this early afternoon in late November had spent the past eight days off loading bodies from U.S. Air Force helicopters. While not as gross as the job of bagging the remains from where they had lain rotting in the unforgiving sun for so many days, this job was still no picnic. The contents of each body bag were in an advanced state of decomposition. They also were not all airtight and the smells of death and the fluids of those who had died ten days before fouled the air and everything in close proximity.

International photojournalists with their still and motion picture cameras mingled with the soldiers as they stood waiting. This moment represented the last chance for them to record the climax of the military mission sent to clean up the biggest mass murder/suicide the modern world had known. Like the GRREG personnel who were in Jonestown bagging the bodies and those here at Timheri whose job it was to place the remains into aluminum coffins, most of these professional news photographers had seen the worst side of humanity and had mastered the art of detaching themselves from the catastrophic events they covered. Nothing seemed to bother these veteran journalists from around the globe.

Clint Yoakum, a lanky white country boy from middle America and Juan Rivera, a still-teenaged young soldier from Puerto Rico, had come to Guyana to record the admission and treatment of any survivors of the tragedy in Jonestown. As medical records specialists, they were simple clerks, more accustomed to carrying a typewriter than a rifle. Unfortunately, the day we arrived in Guyana, we learned that there were no living survivors of the mass suicide/murder that occurred on November 18, 1978. The task force had no need for clerks, but there was a great need for strong arms to lift bodies from helicopters to the trucks waiting to carry them a short distance across the airport tarmac to be placed in coffins bound for Dover, Delaware.

So Yoakum and Rivera had spent their eight days at Timheri Airport shuttling body bags. Day after day they had nothing to look forward to as the awoke in the morning than the back breaking nauseating chore of carrying the dead of Jonestown from one conveyance to another in the sweltering tropical heat.

In the beginning of the operation, the bodies in the bags were of adults, often requiring two men to lift them from the Jolly Green Giant helicopters and carry them to the waiting trucks. When two men are working together, it makes the performance of a painful and difficult task easier. You have someone to talk with, commiserate with and generally pass the time with. But as the days went slowly by, the big bags bore smaller and smaller bodies: the women who had killed their own offspring, then the teens and adolescents and preadolescent who had died before them. For the past two days, the body bags contained toddlers, babies and infants, human remains that were so small, that often three or more were placed into one body bag to conserve the waning supply of bags. Even filled with more than one child, these bags could be easily carried by one person.

When you can perform a job alone and require no immediate assistance from another person, the time you used to fill socializing and communicating with another person is still there and still must be filled. Most of the men working on the Tameri Airport tarmac this final day of the mission filled their work time with daydreams and memories. Their mission for the past week had been to rid helicopters of their rotting human cargo. Many of them had reached their breaking point.

This was not a good time to be working alone, with only your very personal thoughts and recollections of the grossly disturbing scenes and tasks of recent days. Deprived of the opportunity to talk it through with guys who have shared the same nightmare, one can easily become depressed. These men were now doing it alone and in a very real sense, they were <u>going it alone</u>. Although they could not see the contents of the thick dark brown-black bags they were carrying, they knew there were children inside them and their minds took them back to the children who were part of their lives. That can be a heavy psychological burden to bear.

Juan Rivera was a sensitive 18-year-old soldier from Puerto Rico. He had been in the U.S. Army less than six months when he received his first assignment after finishing training. It was to the 601st Medical Company in Panama. He was excited about serving in a Spanish-speaking country.

Less than three months after arriving in the unit, Rivera was spending the fourth week in November of 1978 carrying dead bodies in Guyana. Less than a year after graduating from high school, this teenager was receiving a cruel and totally aberrant initiation into adulthood. And on this final day of the mission, Juan Rivera was carrying some of the final bodies to be evacuated from Jonestown, those of the innocent children who had been murdered on the orders of a totally deranged, would-be savior... the Reverend Jim Jones.

Most of the men carrying the bodies off the helicopters on this day were holding the bags away from their bodies, at arm's length, to avoid the smelly contents from soiling their already dirty beyond cleaning uniforms. Unbelievably, young Rivera was hugging the bags he was removing from the Jolly Green Giant helicopters. He was holding them close to his body and thinking about his baby daughter, Maria, who was less than a year old.

Tears streamed down the cheeks of this emotional young man who sensed the bodies he was bearing were no older than the baby he left behind with his young wife in San Juan. Rivera was walking ghostlike from the helicopter to the truck, the small occupant of the vinyl body bag engulfed in his arms. At the truck, he almost seemed reluctant to deposit his burden and once unencumbered he seemed to move quickly back to the big choppers to once again grab some of the youngest victims of the Jonestown Massacre and almost reverently and lovingly carry them to the waiting truck.

A news photographer noticed Rivera's unique way of transporting these special body bags across the tarmac. He was the only one who seemed to totally disregard the awful odor being emitted from the bags or the vile liquid contents that sometime leaked from them. While the photographer could not have known the young soldier's motivation for acting the way he did, nor could he have understood fully why the proud Puerto Rican father had an expression of severe grief and pain accompanied by copious tears, he did know a great photo opportunity when he saw one.

So the observant photojournalist, armed with an impressive looking Nikon camera, stalked Rivera after he turned from the truck and walked empty handed back to the helicopter with its waiting body bags of babies. As the young Puerto Rican soldier tenderly lifted the next vinyl bag containing a young corpse into his arms and turned, his lips seemed to be moving slightly, as if he was saying a prayer. His eyes were nearly closed, yet tears still streamed unembarrassedly down his ruddy cheeks. His step that had quickened while unburdened by a body bag now became deliberate. It was as if Rivera was trying to communicate with the spirit of the child that once inhabited the body inside the bag he was carrying.

Without an ounce of shame for the intrusion he represented into a young man's private moment, the photographer walked backward in front of the emotion-filled medical records specialist. The lens of his camera less than four feet from Rivera's face and the sound of the motor drive on his Nikon marking the frames being shot of this poignant event. He was intent on catching the stark humanness of Rivera's grief. He wanted the world to see a day from now, a week from now and for all eternity in their newspapers and newsmagazines, what he was viewing live at this moment.

And as Rivera moved slowly toward the truck, with the precious contents of his body bag held tightly against his chest, he didn't acknowledge, nor do I believe he noticed the newsman or his expensive camera mentally assaulting him, invading his most personal painful moment. Neither did I fully comprehend the drama in which Rivera had become a star and which was about to come to a surprise ending.

But Major Major saw what was happening. He was watching it all. He empathized with the grief of the young soldier and despised the crass and uncaring attempt of the photographer to win a Pulitzer Prize. The unorthodox Quartermaster officer was more than angry; he was enraged! He was so incensed at the news photographer's vulgar intrusion into Rivera's private grief that he took a very impulsive and startling step.

Major Major, visibly out of control, raised up the body bag he was carrying and swung it at the unprepared photographer. The bag must have contained a child of about 13 years, or perhaps three younger children whose combined weight would equal that of the average young teen. He lifted the bag high, took a half turn to his right and swung it with great force, striking the totally shocked journalist on the side of the face.

Upon impact, body fluids were expelled from the bag. The expensive black Nikon camera was ripped from the photographer's hands and went crashing to the hot tarmac. The newsman himself fell, landing on his buttocks and joining his damaged camera. Looking up at the obviously mad American Army officer staring intently down at him, the cameraman didn't speak, but the terror in his eyes seemed to ask Major Major why he had hit him.

Major Major stared at the fearful journalist for what seemed like five minutes and then bent down next to him, put his mouth to the reporter's ear and asked quietly, "Man, ain't you got no fuckin' sensitivity?"

The incident with the photojournalist took all of the confident jocularity out of Major Major. He picked up the body bag he had just used as a weapon, carried it to a waiting truck and leaned back and watched me duplicate the same procedure.

As I deposited the body bag I was carrying on the truck, I turned and looked at Major Major. He seemed to regain his composure as quickly as it had originally escaped him. "Who are you anyway?" I asked.

"I'm in charge of the Graves Registration Team," he responded, as if nothing out of the ordinary had just happened. "Want to see where we live?"

Hopping back in the Major's jeep, we drove to a building on the far edge of the tarmac. Hundreds of aluminum coffins, shining brilliantly in the sun, were stacked nearby. I had not seen so many plain metal caskets in one place since the Vietnam War.

As we exited the jeep I quickly became aware of all the flies. While Jonestown had a huge surplus of this pesky common insect, the number at Timheri Airport on this day must have exceeded the population in Jonestown a millionfold.

Suddenly, the entire time I had spent in Guyana seemed like a sick, surreal dream. The stress and unrealness of the past week compressed within my brain and I lost all concept of time or the division of days. Even now, 20 years later, as I recall the incredibly unbelievable events I witnessed there, it is honestly painful and difficult for me to do so. Although I know what I am writing about actually occurred, from this point in time on until we arrived home in Panama some 20 or so hours later, the sequence in which they occurred escapes me.

The flies were incredibly bothersome to me. There were so many of them and there was no defense from their attacks. Not that they caused any pain, they only would land and walk on every portion of your body. And, knowing they had been using the corpses of Jonestown as sustenance and to lay their eggs in, I really didn't want these irritating little creatures touching me.

Four young company grade officers from the GRREG team obviously felt the same way I did. They were sitting in a jeep with several pieces of mosquito netting thrown over it as protection from the flies as they ate their c-ration lunch. But not 30 feet away, on an open bench, sat a bedraggled and totally unkempt specialist fourth class. He also was eating his lunch, but without benefit of insect netting.

Like the corpses in Jonestown, the tired young soldier's entire body was covered with flies. Hundreds of them buzzed around, landing and taking off from every part of him, walking on his bare arms, hands and face with impunity and completely without any sign of objection from the specialist. Flies covered the can from which he was eating, walking in and out of it without the least sign of repugnance from the diner. Instead of shooing the flies away, he seemed oblivious to their presence, maybe even willing to share his simple meal with these insects.

The smell at Timheri Airport was much worse than the odor in Jonestown. At least in Jonestown it rained daily and there was the green of the jungle that must have provided some tropical fragrances that provided at least a modicum of natural deodorizor to the putrefying smell of the decomposing bodies. There were no trees near the airport in Georgetown. There was no soil for the body fluids to seep into, only hot black tarmac that cooked and dried the awful smelling secretions.

Full body bags waiting to be placed in coffins were stacked some 25 yards from where the nonchalant GRREG specialist was sharing his lunch with the flies. The awful odors and presence of the dead did not disturb his appetite any more than the creatures that were stealing his meal. He steadily enjoyed eating the Army food.

Suddenly Major Major noticed something was amiss. I had not picked up on it, but did as soon as the Quartermaster officer asked the soldier a question.

"James, what's that body bag doing there under the bench?" the major forcefully inquired.

The young man, not missing a beat, took a bite of his food, looked up at Major Major and matter-of-factly stated, "Taking it home for a souvenir sir."

"James, pick that body bag up and put it where it belongs," barked Major Major.

The GRREG specialist with the desire to take a piece of Jonestown home with him, shrugged his shoulders with resignation, put the plastic spoon into his nearly empty can of c-rations, placed the can on the bench, stood and grasped the offending body bag with both hands and dragged it over to where the others were laying.

When he returned back to the bench, the GRREG man sat down, picked up his food, watched as a dozen or so flies flew out of its open top and then resumed his interrupted meal.

“These are my men,” said Major Major, “They do a good job, but sometimes, some of them act a little weird.”

"The world rolls round forever like a mill;
It grinds out death and life and good and ill;
It has no purpose, heart or mind or will."

James Thompson

Eleven

Party Animals

By 1600 hours, I was gratefully reunited with Samuels, Fields, our Air Force communications men and two Army fuel specialists. Sanders was also able to join us and was almost back to full strength after receiving two liters of fluids by intravenous infusion. Our little group that had been fairly isolated during the entire mission, sat together in the huge abandoned terminal building that had become the headquarters for the Joint Task Force.

We were soon joined by Captain Snow, Major Buenos and Specialists Rivera and Yoakum. The Army fuel specialists and Air Force communications men said their goodbyes and went to rejoin their respective units as did others who also had their units split up during the operation. All the different groups were gathered together and seemed to be doing essentially the same thing ours was... decompressing after the most stressful week of our lives.

The scenario seemed to be the same with each individual group of servicemen and women. At first, upon joining together, they greeted one another and took their places sitting on their personal gear. For the first hour or so, most smoked cigarettes and stared into space. Very little chatter could be heard from these pods of people that occupied the expansive terminal building. They stared, they smoked, they apparently contemplated the awful events and scenes they had witnessed and participated in over the past several days in silence, trying to make some personal sense of a tragedy of such enormous proportions, they could not even have contemplated it until they actually participated in it.

Then slowly, almost imperceptibly, conversation seemed to grow. First there were simple rhetorical statements made one at a time by members of the groups, said to no one in particular. There was no order in which members of units spoke and there apparently was no specific individual to whom the comments were directed. People simply said whatever thoughts happened to be occupying their tired brains at the moment. It was as if by verbalizing what was inside them they were testing the waters to see if the same ideas were shared by others around them. There was no cohesion to the phrases being made. The words were not in response to what was vocalized by another person.

It was like bullfrogs sitting around a pond as the sun goes down. Before the day begins to fade, the pond is silent, the creatures of the night just awakening from their day of sleep. Soon, as darkness begins to fall, one frog emits a familiar "ribit". There is a long pause and from another lily pad comes another "ribit," seemingly unrelated to the first. Then other frogs in other parts of the pond can be heard adding their unrelated "ribits" to the flow of sounds. Before long, the entire area is alive with a cacophony of unrelated frog talk.

Members of our team made their individual comments. There was a pause. Then someone else would add an apparently unrelated verbal contribution and then a third person would verbalize his or her feelings.

Before long, even the shyest, most introverted soldier was speaking his mind, even if he was speaking it to no one in particular.

This oral exercise soon became cathartic. As a group, we had all experienced different feelings and had various reactions and responses to what we had seen, heard and done over the past week. We were a lot like the soldier who had watched his friend die horribly and violently before his eyes in the track vehicle accident in Panama. At first we could not talk about it because it was totally foreign to the comfortable, normal experiences of everyday life. It was like a horrible nightmare that we had lived through these last several days. We slowly and individually contemplated our experience, then began to verbalize our feelings, if only to ourselves. Soon we all opened up and were sharing our private experiences and thoughts, embellishing them and adding to the comments of others until we were able to face the awfulness of the past week in a therapeutic manner.

The beer and rum that was provided by the State Department, while meant to create an atmosphere of celebration, actually facilitated conversation, by allowing us to let our guard down. While not intended for this purpose, the alcohol actually was, in a way, medicinal and helped us face the reality of what we had seen and experienced.

No one knew what time we would be leaving Timheri Airport. We had been told that the Air Force was on their way to remove us from this place of death to the land of normalcy from whence we had come on the 19th of November. By 1800 hours, the entire force except for the Graves Registration team had completed their mission, were packed and ready to leave and were well into consuming the beverages that had been provided us. However, while the GRREG soldiers still had another day of work to perform before they too could go home, they were given the night off and joined us in partaking of the alcoholic spirits. The booze, in a very real way, chased the spirits of Jonestown's dead from our memories, at least for the time being.

Recollections of this final night in Guyana are less than vivid. When you are physically tired, very little alcohol is needed to make you forget the bad things you have experienced. My mind is muddled by the mixture of beer and rum and a very concerted effort that was made to repress the memories of a time in my life that was extremely destructive to my normal positive psyche.

Every member of the Joint Task Force that came from the 193rd Infantry Brigade in Panama indulged in the booze that flowed so freely that night. The more we drank the more we forgot and the rowdier we became. A week's worth of unbelievable stress was relieved by half an evenings' worth of drinking. Personally, I feel this was the best medicine for the bad disease to which we all had been exposed to.

By 2200 hours, the beverages were, for the most part consumed, except for the full souvenir bottles of Banks Beer and DM Gold Label Rum many of us packed away to take home. The majority of our contingent of nearly 200 soldiers were either asleep or close to it because of the shear physical exhaustion the work of the past week brought on, or were nearly anesthetized by the alcohol we had consumed.

My Brigade Surgeon, Major Buenos, sat in a chair next to me. He was nodding off, fighting the effects of too much rum and not enough sleep. I noticed he had a wooden crate in the seat next to him that I did not see when we arrived in Guyana.

"What's in the box, Doc?" I asked, trying to make conversation.

"Shhhh," said Buenos, putting two fingers to his lips. "It's a microscope. I liberated it from Jonestown."

The infirmary in Jonestown had a very sophisticated and expensive training microscope with two eye pieces. Buenos decided that since everyone in the commune was dead he would add this item to his personal inventory of medical equipment.

I don't believe Major Buenos considered the procurement of this instrument worth thousands of dollars as stealing. After all, the military has a long history of obtaining needed supplies that were difficult to get through what is euphemistically called a "midnight requisition."

When I was in Vietnam our evacuation hospital had "procured" air conditioners for our wards through similar unorthodox and imaginative means. The people of Jonestown no longer had a need for this training microscope, but Doctor Buenos did. So he took it. This was to be the catalyst for an upcoming witch hunt by the Army's Criminal Investigation Division in Panama that would involve every person from the 193rd Infantry Brigade who was part of the Joint Task Force.

While Major Buenos and I were discussing his acquisition of a new piece of medical equipment for the brigade surgeon's office, two C-130s arrived from Howard Air Force Base for the flight home. The big birds taxied from the runway to just outside the old terminal building in which we were waiting. The crews shut down their big engines and within a few minutes they walked into the terminal. The two colonels who were in command of the aircraft seemed startled and shocked by what they saw.

Here were nearly 200 military personnel who were obviously far from being fit to fight and most assuredly, by Air Force standards, unfit for flight.. The odor being emitted from most of us was extremely disgusting to the uninitiated and these pilots were not part of our exclusive club. The fact that most of us were obviously displaying the effects of too much alcoholic consumption did not seem to bring joy to the faces of these two stern Air Force officers. I heard one of them ask loudly, "Who is in charge here?"

A slightly drunk Colonel Gordon, using all the strength he could muster at the time, stood up slowly and walked toward the sober Air Force officers with as much dignity and control as he could summon. "I am in charge," he announced for all to hear.

"We can't fly this bunch of drunks in U.S. Air Force aircraft," the senior of the two pilots unequivocally stated.

"You not only can, you will," said Colonel Gordon with as much force as his Air Force counterpart. The two stood staring at each other for some time. Then I saw Colonel Gordon take the irate Air Force officer aside. They sat down and seemed to have a serious and earnest conversation.

Later I learned that Colonel Gordon related to the Air Force pilot all the terrible and stressful experiences we had gone through over the past week. He told them that although we all were, for the most part, in no condition to "make a movement," he would brief all of us and insure we behaved properly during the five hour flight back to Panama. The Air Force colonel seemed skeptical, but he did consult with the crews of both aircraft. After talking once again with Colonel Gordon, it appeared the decision was made to carry us all back home despite our collective sloven and drunken condition.

Colonel Gordon called the noncommissioned officers in charge of each unit together for a briefing. He explained that the Air Force had a strict regulation that all passengers on their aircraft must be sober. While he had admitted to the ranking pilot that very few, if any of his charges fit that description, he would ensure that everyone behaved in an appropriate and professional manner. Now Colonel Gordon was directing the NCOs of the brigade to make sure his promise to the reluctant Air Force pilot was kept.

I was fortunate, with only with only five enlisted men and two officers to worry about, my group was smaller than most. Major Buenos and Captain Snow were officers and gentlemen and I expected they would have no problem displaying the proper demeanor during the trip. In fact, Captain Snow was actually sober. Major Buenos was fairly well inebriated, but he held his liquor well.

My enlisted personnel were all extremely well lubricated by the Guyana beer and rum that they had so liberally consumed over the past few hours. The hardest task that I faced in helping Colonel Gordon keep his promise to the Air Force was to get these five people safely on the aircraft. Once there, I was certain they all would sleep very well until we touched down at Howard Air Force Base.

Sanders had been sleeping for some time and once I was able to fully awaken him, he became a very capable escort for Specialist 6 Ben Samuels who was the most unsteady of our group. Sanders was much bigger than Samuels and had no trouble getting him and his gear into the C-130. My fellow clinical specialist was soon belted securely into a seat and he quickly resumed the deep sleep he had been enjoying before being aroused to walk out to the aircraft.

Rivera would have won the prize for being the most unsteady, but he was so drunk he could not be aroused. Yoakum and I actually carried the little medical records specialist onto the plane and secured his seat belt. Both he and Samuels snored loudly throughout the entire five hour flight. Fields was able to ambulate to the aircraft under his own power and he also slept throughout the flight. Captain Snow, Specialist Four Yoakum and I accompanied Major Buenos onto the C-130, the officer and specialist on either side of the physician, with me carrying the liberated microscope bringing up the rear.

To the credit of the men and women who made that flight from Timheri Airport to Howard Air Force Base that November 27, 1978, everyone behaved themselves very well. I do not remember seeing anyone upchuck and there was absolutely no rowdy behavior displayed during the entire trip. The five hours in the air did have some interesting moments however.

Combat C-130s do not have rest rooms on board. There is a tube toward the rear of the aircraft with a funnel-like device sticking out of it that is called a “piss tube.” This device was designed specifically with male servicemen in mind. Unfortunately, there were four female soldiers on our flight and these women had consumed great amounts of beer. As every medic and most other people know, this beverage is an excellent diuretic and the piss tube was a popular gathering place for soldiers on this long trip.

Even the females who were not equipped with anatomical features that the piss tube was originally designed for, used it with little or no difficulty and although the procedure involved them dropping their trousers, they did so unabashedly and without any lewd or uncalled for remarks by the opposite sex on the flight.

Another interesting phenomenon that occurred shortly after take off was that many of the passengers released their seat belts and lay down on top of palletized equipment so they could get a more restful sleep. Some slept in the jeep that was on board. Since we encountered no turbulence of any consequence during the flight to Panama, this was not really a problem, although it did take us some time to wake up everyone and get them strapped in for the landing at Howard Air Force Base.

Unbeknownst to any of us on the two C-130s that returned from the Joint Humanitarian Task Force to Jonestown, Guyana early that morning of November 28, 1978, General K.C. Luer, the new 193rd Infantry Brigade Commanding General had prepared a somewhat elaborate ceremony on the tarmac of Howard Air Force Base to mark our return. The Army band was present and playing when the rear doors to the big C-130s opened that dark morning. The general himself was standing on a makeshift stand with a podium, waiting to give our group words of congratulations for a mission well done.

What no one who planned the reception had anticipated was the condition of the participants of this thoroughly repugnant and disgusting mission. All of us, while not aware of the odor ourselves, smelled extremely bad to noses that had not been exposed to the aroma of death for the past week. This included the band members who quickly seemed to catch a whiff of our "Jonestown Perfume" and lost the ability to perform the march music they had practiced for the past week without gagging or even puking.

While General Luer himself did not seem to mind making his speech under these adverse conditions, the honorees were less than prepared to listen to him. Not only did we smell bad, we were tired, hung over, hadn't shaved in a week and wanted no more than to get home to a bath tub and our loved ones.

Every member of the Joint Task Force being honored by General Luer, his entourage and band that early morning, stumbled out of the aircraft unceremoniously and made their way into the terminal. Inside, we quickly became the building's only occupants as the Air Force personnel assigned to Howard Air Force Base evacuated to the outdoors and fresh air. General Luer, made a few comments as we passed by him, then stood in behind the podium on the portable platform with a shocked stare on his face.

The party was over and the hard job of telling our friends and families about our experience was about to begin. Every one of us who had participated in this mission had changed in some way and our lives after Jonestown would never be the same as before.

Twelve

The Party's Over

While Samuels and the other members of my team saw to the off loading of our equipment and supplies, I went to a telephone to call the Charge of Quarters of the 601st Medical Company so he could dispatch a vehicle to Howard Air Force Base to transport us back to the unit. It was around 0330 hours. Sanders was the unit armorer and we didn't have access to the arms rooms since he accompanied our team to Guyana. I asked the CQ who had the keys to the arms room. He told me that the company's executive officer, Lieutenant Canasta had them.

"Well, please call Lieutenant Canasta and let him know we are back so we can turn in our weapons when we get to the company," I directed the CQ. He said he would call the XO and pass the word.

Canasta was not my favorite officer and I was not his favorite noncom. We had a run-in the year before when he became the officer in charge of the my ambulance platoon at Fort Gulick. He was a very strict authoritarian leader, without the sense of humor necessary to make men do things that they don't want to do and do them well. He was very conservative; a staunch and stodgy Roman Catholic originally from Central America and with the habit of making rash decisions that were usually wrong.

About a half an hour after I first talked with the CQ, a follow-up call assured us the vehicle should be arriving at Howard Air Force Base any minute. Before terminating the call, I asked the CQ if Lieutenant Canasta had arrived at the company.

"He told me he'd be in at 0800 hours and you all are to wait here for his arrival," said the CQ.

"He what?!" I asked incredulously. The CQ repeated what the XO had told him, adding that Canasta was upset at having been awoken from a sound sleep.

"Give me his phone number," I ordered the junior noncom who was on duty as charge of quarters that night. He reluctantly complied.

I quickly called Lieutenant Canasta and got the irritating young officer on the line. "Good morning Lieutenant, hope I didn't disturb your beauty sleep," I said snidely.

"Who is this?" inquired the arrogant XO.

"This is Specialist Six Brailey, just back from Jonestown, Guyana with five men who need to turn in their weapons and get home to take a bath," I replied lightly, "I expect you will be in the company before we get back from Howard. We are leaving in about ten minutes."

"I told the CQ I'll be in a 0800 hours and that's when I'll be in there," stated Canasta.

"Listen you sorry excuse for an officer, I've always thought you were a f***ed up a**hole and you are proving it right now," I shouted. "As far as I am concerned you are an arrogant little snot who wouldn't make a pimple on a decent NCO's ass. We are tired, hung over and we don't need any s**t from an a**hole the likes of you!"

"WHAT DID YOU SAY?" screamed Canasta into the phone.

"You heard me you insipid weasel. You'd better hope we never go to war because you'll have to be dodging bullets from both sides you f***!" I taunted. "You are such a sorry excuse for an officer that I didn't expect you to drag your sorry ass into the company at this hour. We all know what you are, now you have proven it! YOU SUCK!!" I concluded forcefully.

"I'LL SEE YOUR ASS IN THE ORDERLY ROOM MISTER!!" Canasta spitted into the telephone. I quietly hung the receiver of my phone up and smiled. "The XO says he'll meet us in the orderly room fellas," I announced to my troops who were staring at me with astonished looks on their faces.

Our 2 1/2 ton truck pulled up in front of the company day room. I told the driver to secure the vehicle in the motor pool and to go to bed. We would unload our equipment the next day.

The rest of the team had picked up their personal gear and stowed it against the building. We already had decided that since it smelled so bad, no one was likely to steal it. Then we walked into the dayroom as a group.

Lieutenant Canasta was awaiting our arrival. His face was beet red and he seemed to be having a difficult time controlling his rage. The keys to the arms room were in his left hand. I walked right up to the angry junior officer, stood at attention, rendered a proper salute with my right hand and took the keys from him with my left.

"Thank you for bringing the arms room keys in at such an early hour, Lieutenant," I said as I snapped a salute with my right hand and threw the arms room keys to Sanders with my left. "Open the arms room up and collect the weapons," I ordered Sanders and he and the rest of the team went downstairs.

"Would you care to repeat what you said to me on the phone to my face?" asked a barely under control Lieutenant Canasta.

"No sir, I don't think so. My words served their purpose and there is no need to repeat them," I stated calmly to the fuming XO.

"What?! Aren't you brave enough to say them? Don't you have balls enough to say them?" screamed the young officer as he tried to goad me into disrespecting him in front of witnesses.

"Like I said, there is no need to now..." I started to respond.

"You are nothing!! yelled the lieutenant. "You are nothing!!" he shouted, unable to find a vocabulary greater than that of a fifth grader or to put more than three words together in a sentence.

"Well, if you feel that way about it," I said in a building voice and paused. Quickly the CQ and his runner, catching the reason for my hesiitation, left the room, closing the big metal fire doors behind them. "If you feel that way about it," I continued calmly and in low voice, "You ARE a f***ing a**hole!"

The totally insulted XO looked around the room to ascertain the identity of any witnesses. When he didn't see any, the thoroughly defeated lieutenant, spun around and strode toward the orderly room in long determined strides. As soon as he was gone, the CQ and his runner, peaked from behind the door on the other side of the room.

"What got into you?" asked the Charge of Quarters. "Oh," I replied, "the only way I could get that a**hole to come in here and open the arms room was to make him crazy when I called him on the phone. I beat him and he knows it."

"Man, you'd better go and apologize," said the timid CQ. "You are probably right," I replied, walking toward the orderly room.

As I entered the hall where the company offices were, I saw Lieutenant Canasta sitting behind his desk, feverishly writing on a yellow legal pad. I knew he was writing me up and savoring every minute of it to the enth degree. It seemed almost a shame to interrupt the obvious fun the XO was having composing his report of my disrespect and insubordination. But interrupt his revery I did!

I calmly approached the front of the XO's standard government issue metal desk, stood straight and stiff at attention and rendered and held a proper military salute. "Specialist Brailey wishes to apologize for his disrespectful behavior Lieutenant," I announced. "I said a lot of things to you on the phone that I knew would upset you and cause you to come into the company so I could get the arms room keys. I know it was wrong, but I was tired and hung over and in dire need of a bath,"

I would have continued, but as I stood there, making my apology, holding my right hand up to my forehead in a salute, the lieutenant continued his furious scribbling and totally refused to acknowledge my presence. Seeing I was getting no where with this prim little sissy of an officer, I dropped my salute, bent down toward his body hunched over his desk and said slowly and deliberately, "But if you aren't man enough to accept my apology, the 'f***ing a**hole' still stands!"

I did an about face, left the orderly room area and went to the arms room to turn in my weapon. While down there, Sanders told me not to worry, no one heard what I had said to the XO and even if they did, they wouldn't go against me. I wasn't so sure, When Canasta was a second lieutenant I had really pissed him off and now he was the company XO and I had antagonized him again. I was a little worried that I was letting the ice get a little too thin under my feet.But, after I turned in my weapon, went home to my family and took a bath, I called First Sergeant Phil Arthur to get his advice.

The sun was just rising in Panama when I called Top that Sunday morning. He was glad we were back home and told me to come over to his quarters to drink a beer. I related the events of the early morning hours, he told me to forget they ever happened and not to worry. I don't know what Phil Arthur had on Lieutenant Canasta, but the incidents of disrespect and insubordination were never mentioned again.

At his point in the narrative, I feel compelled to relate the first run-in I had with Canasta when he was a second lieutenant and newly assigned to the company. It has nothing to do with the story, but it is funny and true. After I tell you this story, there is a classic Lieutenant Canasta story that begs to be told and then I promise, I will get back to the subject of this book. But up to now, this has been a pretty heavy book and a little real levity instead of the horror and dark humor of the GRREG team seems in order.

When Canasta was first assigned to the 601st Medical Company, the commander sent him to Fort Gulick to replace Lieutenant Bragg as platoon leader of the Atlantic Platoon, an ambulance platoon that had been formed to provide medical support to units at Forts Sherman, Davis and Gulick on the Atlantic side of the Canal Zone, some 55 miles away from where the rest of the company was located at Fort Clayton. Bragg was a very likeable officer, who was comfortable around all kinds of people. This made him a great platoon leader.

Canasta was the exact antithesis of Bragg. Bragg

was a jovial extrovert. Canasta was a shy and stern introvert. Bragg was flexible and understanding. Canasta was extremely rigid and not at all tolerant. Bragg had a 'live and let live' attitude and for Canasta it was 'my way or the highway.'

The Atlantic Platoon was made up of the dregs of the company: soldiers the old first sergeant and company commander wanted to get out from under the flag pole. But, the two senior soldiers of the company had not announced their intentions of sending all the dope smokers and hard cases to the Atlantic Platoon when they asked for volunteers to be Platoon Leader and Sergeant. It was right after Lieutenant Bragg and I volunteered for the jobs that the rest of the members of the platoon were chosen. With the exception of the motor sergeant, every person selected was undesirable. Two were homosexuals, several were marijuana smokers, most were disciplinary problem-prone.

But Bragg and I developed a good team. We used positive reinforcement and mutual respect and developed a group of guys who worked well together. Our softball and bowling teams were the "Misfits." But we showed these soldiers who had never fit in before that they had value and worth and made them into a productive cohesive unit.

Then Lieutenant Canasta came along. Bragg was promoted to first lieutenant and was called back to the company to be the XO. Canasta had just arrived from the States and was a new officer. He objected to my choice of Physical Training Leader.

Sid Flecks was a thin black soldier with the body of a ballet dancer and the temperament to match. His speech and body language all said he was gay and Sid didn't care who was listening. At a time when homosexuality in the military was considerably more taboo than it is now, Sid lived his life the way he wanted, without pretense or fear.

Every morning we would sit in the day room waiting for Sid to come downstairs and take us outside for morning Physical Training. He would wear outrageous outfits, pink tights, purple spandex shirts. He'd lead all 23 of us all male soldiers outside for our morning exercises with a "Let's go girls, time for PT," yelled in a shrill faggoty soprano voice.

After three days of observing Sid's effeminate antic, Canasta called me into his office. "This guy Fleck," asked the stuffed shirt of a lieutenant, "is he, is he, is he a little... funny?"

"Oh, sir, we all think he's hilarious," was my reply.

"Uh, no, maybe you don't understand, Specialist Brailey, what I want to know is, uh, is Fleck, uh, is he gay?" asked the conservative Canasta, groping for words.

"Well sir, he's happy all the time." I stated brightly.

By now, the new platoon leader realized I was playing with him. "Specialist Six Brailey, I want to know if Fleck is a homosexual," the no nonsense but foolish lieutenant said.

Never one to do anything halfway, I responded with, "Well, sir, I can't speak with any authority about his sexual preferences, but if you are looking for a partner, I'll ask him."

Canasta locked my heels. "Stand at attention when I am talking to you soldier!" he shouted. "I don't want any damn faggots in my platoon. Do you understand me? I don't want any goddman faggots in my platoon! Now, is Fleck a faggot or not?"

I looked the bigoted lieutenant straight in the eye

and said, "Sir, I have never seen Fleck hold hands with a man or kiss on a man or behave in any inappropriate way with a man. Sure he's a little strange. He talks in a high voice. He has effeminate mannerisms. But there is nothing in the Army Regs against being strange that I know of. Fleck runs 15 miles every other day, maxes his PT test and his MOS test, takes better care of his ambulance than any other man in the platoon and is always willing to do the job when asked. And Lieutenant Canasta," I said deliberately, "Fleck is one of the best soldiers I ever worked with and if you do anything to make me lose him, you will regret it."

The lieutenant didn't realize it, but there was an open transom over his door and half the platoon was sitting in the day room outside his office at the time of our dialogue. When I made my last statement, a great cheer went up in the day room and Canasta realized he was outnumbered. He didn't bother discussing Fleck again.

Lieutenant Canasta, besides every thing else he was, was a shy prude. When the unit was in the field, he would be the last one down to the portable shower facility at night to take his daily bath. It was made of two 55-gallon drums on a seven foot wooden stand.

By the time he had made executive officer, Canasta had alienated all of the enlisted personnel and most of the officers in the 601st Medical Company. He was about as well-liked as case of the "Black Syph."

One night, after the soldiers of the company had endured about as much as they could stand of this prissy officer, one of the NCOs who had several run ins with him since the time he first arrived in the company, emptied all of the water from one of the drums at the shower point. Then he emptied all but about five gallons from the other drum and put two pints of a chemical reagent, methylene blue into the drum.

About twenty minutes later, Lieutenant Canasta made his way down to the unlit shower area and bathed until the water ran out of the drum. He then dried off and went back to the small tent he shared with three other male lieutenants. Methylene blue is odorless... But not colorless. For the next two weeks, until it completely wore off, Lieutenant Canasta's skin was a bright blue hue. While his skin was blue for only a couple of weeks, for the rest of his assignment in the 601st Medical Company, the name "Lieutenant Smurf" <u>never</u> wore off.

First Sergeant Phil Arthur had saved my butt on several occassions. I first served under him as a young private first class in Vietnam. My indiscretion with

Lieutenant Canasta was the last time he ever had to perform such a service for me.

A few days after returning from Guyana, Arthur called me into his office. It was around 1000 hours in the morning. He looked at me quizzically and asked if I or my guys had done anything wrong when we were on the Joint Task Force. Having had already briefed him on the sexual exploits of the young studs on my team in Matthews Ridge I asked if that might be the subject of the inquiry. Top said that he was doubtful. Then he proceeded to inform me that our team's presence was required at the local Army Criminal Investigation Division office at Albrook Air Base.

The guys and I loaded into a gamma goat ambulance and drove to the CID office. When we arrived, most of the other soldiers from the 193rd Infantry Brigade that had been sent to Guyana were sitting on the lawn outside the building. No one knew why we were there. We reported in at the office and were told to join everyone else outside. We sat and waited as names were called and one at a time, our fellow task force members went inside.

Before long, it was my turn to be called. Upon entering the main door I was met by a CID agent wearing fatigues with the familiar "US" insignia placed where every other soldier in the Army wore their insignia of rank. He directed me into a small room with a table and three chairs. Another CID agent was waiting for us in the room.

The two introduced themselves but did not divulge the reason we all had been called together at the CID office. Then I was read my rights under Article 32 of the Uniform Code of Military Justice. The words started out with the familiar, "You have the right to remain silent..." The two inquisitors seemed to accept my response that I had no problem answering their questions because there had been no illegal activities for which to fear for reprisals.

"Did you bring anything back from Guyana that you did not take there with you?" questioned the CID agent who had met me in the outer office.

"Yes, a bottle of Banks Beer and a bottle of DM Gold Label Rum, a can of mixed nuts, a can of Fritos and some photographs," was my honest reply.

The ears of the second CID agent pricked up when he heard the word "photographs." "Where did you get these photographs?" was his question. The story as to the acquisition of the twenty Poloroid pictuers purchased from the young Guyanese man in the bar in Matthews Ridge was the truth. Thus, the incident was accurately related to the CID interogators.

"Are you sure you did not steal these photos from Jonestown?" I was asked. "Quite sure," was my immediate and forceful response..

"What are these pictures of?" the curious CID man asked. I told him about the party the young man said he was invited to and said I had paid him ten American dollars for the photos and had gotten a receipt.

"Where are these pictures now?" I was asked. Tiring of their game, I decided to stretch the truth a bit and said, "I mailed all but one to my stepfather yesterday and told him to try to sell them to Newsweek."

"Why did you keep that one picture?" "Because I felt it had no commercial value." "We want to see the picture." "It's at my quarters, I'll go over there and bring it back," went our volly of words back and forth.

"No," said the CID man, "We will take you to get it." And the two men with "U.S." instead of rank on their collar accompanied me to a CID sedan and drove me to my house. When we walked to the front door, I unlocked it and stepped inside. The two agents tried to follow me but

but I told them I would not allow them into my home unless they had a warrant. The agents remained outside as I entered my home, locked the door, proceeded to my bedroom and extracted a photo of an unknown person looking at a beehive. The photo, along with the receipt given me by the Guyanese young man was all that was required to defuse the problem.

Upon returning to the CID office, the two agents took the photo and receipt, replacing them with a receipt of their own. I was told I could leave.

Information came to my attention that several of the task force members were being forced to return brochures and campaign style buttons of Reverend Jim Jones that they had picked up as souvenirs in Jonestown.

This angered me. Relief was just across the Panama Canal at the Staff Judge Advocate's Office. After providing facts concerning the witch hunt that the CID was conducting, one brave captain attorney called the CID commander and suggested he stop this illegal search immediately. The search was stopped and all of us got our innocuous souvenirs back, all of us except Major Buenos, who had to turn in his microscope.

Months went by. In 1979, the soldiers and American residents of Panama were more interested in the Panama Canal Zone Treaty than what had happened in Jonestown. Those of us who had participated in the bizarre mission tried to dismiss the horrible memories associated with the savage massacre. Try as one might, the indelible recollections of that haunting experience are not easily repressed.

Then, in November 1979, as I passed by the bakery in Balboa, Panama one Sunday morning, the overpowering sweet smell of freshly made pastries enveloped me. I began to perspire and then to shake and before I knew it, I was vomiting on the sidewalk. For you see, the sweet smell of the bakery, that I had been enjoying at least once a week for the past several years, on this morning in November 1979, reminded me of the odor emitted from the 914 bodies that littered Jonestown a year before.

I made my way home as quickly as possible after the nauseating experience at the bakery. For the next week or so my life was a shambles. It was difficult to sleep at night and when sleep finally came, it was filled with nightmares. My screams woke my wife and children several times that third week of November 1979.

My relationship with my wife and children was strained during this time. I was unusually moody and emotional. Then, as quickly as they struck, these unusual emotional experiences went away. The rest of the year went on uneventfully. In the summer of 1980 I was transferred to Fort Sill, Oklahoma. Life was good. I enjoyed fishing in the nearby wildlife refuge and liesure times with my wife and children; until mid November, when I started getting weird again.

Not realizing it at the time, I was a victim... I was plagued with what some psychologists term "anniversary syndrome." Psychologists refer to it as a type of post-traumatic stress disorder that visits its victims during the anniversary of some exquisite and disturbing trauma in their life. It was several years later that a psychiatrist who attended our church helped by explaining that this bizarre behavior is not unusual. What we experienced in Guyana was so horrific... so removed from the norm, that the mind cannot completely accept the reality of what actually transpired.

The helpful psychiatrist stressed the importance of placing everything in perspective and accepting the fact that the tragic event is history... not the present, and certainly not the future. Knowing that and being able to process it intellectually is two different things however. The sign that hung over Reverend Jim Jones' rostrum in the Pavillion in Jonestown flashes in my memory... "Those who do not remember the past are condemned to repeat it."

The Jonestown Tragedy has had a profound effect on my life. I was raised in a Baptist home by a mother who still, in my fiftieth year, attends the same church she and I grew up in. But church is something I am suspicious of now. For me it isn't a place of peace and solace but a potential cause of pain and suffering. I have become suspect and cynical, not trusting churchmen and finding my distrust being validated when someone my mother respects, like Jimmy Swaggart or Jim Baker, falls.

I am still haunted by the ghosts of November. While they do not cause me to behave strangely or lose sleep during the anniversary month of their deaths anymore, they affect me nevertheless. My faith will never quite be the same as it was before they left this earth forcing me to become part of their afterlives. Having spent two tours in Vietnam during some of the worst fighting of the war I know we can perservere through the worst of circumstances. However, those 635 days spent in a combat zone as a medic watching my fellow soldiers lose limbs and die were no where near as traumatic to me as the nine days in that Twighlight Zone known as Jonestown in 1978.

Epilogue

Nineteen Novembers have passed since that fateful period in 1978 in which 914 Americans perished. Much has been written about the Peoples Temple, Jim Jones and the way he and his flock lived and died. No less than a dozen sites can be found on the World Wide Web that are dedicated to Jonestown and the tragedy that occurred in that forbidding jungle. The most scholarly and objective website is Alternative Considerations of Jonestown and Peoples Temple by the Department of Philosophy and Religion at the University of North Dakota. It can be found at *www.und.nodak.edu/dept/philrel/jonestown.*

Rebecca Moore, a professor of Religion at that institution is the author and co-editor of five books on the Peoples Temple. Ms. Moore lost two sisters and a nephew in the Jonestown Massacre. After the remains of her loved ones and the other American Jonestown victims were returned to Dover, Delaware, Ms. Moore and her family had some extremely difficult experiences in dealing with the United States government. An excerpt of her essay, "Last Rights" can be found in the Appendix.

While the mass suicides/murders at Jonestown were the largest, most horrendous in modern human history, they were the precursor to several similar events on a smaller scale. On December 13, 1990, 12 people died in a religious ritual in Tijuana, Mexico after drinking fruit punch tainted with industrial alcohol. A year later, Mexican minister Ramon Morales Almazan and 29 followers suffocated after he told them to keep praying and to ignore toxic fumes that were filling his church.

In October 1993, 53 Vietnamese tribal villagers committed mass suicide with flintlock guns and other primitive weapons in the belief they would go straight to heaven. They apparently were victims of a scam perpetrated by a man who received cash donations from the group for promising them a speedy road to paradise. On April 19, 1993, 84 Branch Davidians led by David Koresh, died in a fire and shootout with out of control federal agents in Waco, Texas, ending a 51-day siege of their cult compound.

The Solar Temple is a bizarre international sect that believes ritualized suicide leads to rebirth on a planet named Sirius. In October 1994, the burned bodies of 48 Solar Temple members were discovered in a farmhouse and three separate chalets in Switzerland. At the same time, five other bodies, including an infant's were found in a house north of Montreal. In December 1995, 16 Solar Temple members were found dead in a burned house outside Grenoble, in the French Alps. On March 23, 1997, the charred bodies of three women and two men were found inside a house in Saint Casimir, Quebec. All were members of the Solar Temple.

Finally, on March 26, 1997 the bodies of 39 men were discovered in a mass suicide near San Diego. These members of Heaven's Gate also believed their deaths would lead to rebirth and a future life with aliens.

As the Millennium approaches, many experts predict there will be an upsurge in cult related deaths and suicides. It is difficult for me to believe that any of these impending events will be as bizarre and awful as the Jonestown Massacre of November 18, 1978.

It has been 20 years since the ghosts of November

became an unwelcome part of my life. For a long time, after learning the cause of this "anniversary syndrome," I was able to control them and keep them from bothering me. But as the anniversary of this monumental tragedy approaches, these very troublesome entities have returned, causing me to once again start losing sleep and experience nightmares.

While doing research for this book in the summer of 1998, an extensive search was made to secure an appropriate photo to use on the cover jacket. Briefly, consideration was given to an extremely graphic photo depicting the widespread mass of bloated bodies near the Pavilion. It would have been totally insensitive to the survivors and family members to use such a photo.

Through the urgings of my wife, Jessie Philips-Brailey and family members of three victims, Rebecca Moore and her husband, I decided to use photos of some of the people who perished in Jonestown that depict happy times in their lives. Even these images, as peaceful as they seem, trouble me deeply as I think about what became of the men, women and children depicted in the photos.

The site of that unbelievable carnage has robbed me of sleep again and again! The inescapable memories of those eight days of hell continue to haunt me. Imagine being fearful of sleep... sleep that conjures up grotesque dreams that take me back to a vivid nightmare I actually lived twenty years ago.

This book has taken me two decades to write. I have tried to put the events of that period of my life on a shelf way in the back of my brain. But circumstances and anniversaries won't allow me that luxery. This book has reluctantly been written in order to share with others some of the unbelievable experiences we encountered in Guyana nearly so long ago. Hopefully it will be helpful in granting some measure of closure for the countless number of folks whose lives have been tragically impacted by the sorid events of Jonestown, Guyana.

The names of all of the members of my team and some of the other key players in this story have been changed. However, each character in this book is a real person and the events described really happened. Those men I served with in Guyana will recognize themselves. I hope they find the depictions accurate.

Epilogue

The GRREG soldiers have a terrible job and a near-sacred responsibility and they perform their duties admirably. I forgive them their little quirks and hope the reader is so inclined to follow suit.

The characters depicted in this book are human. So too are the readers that now share the knowledge of the senseless and tragic loss of 914 American citizens because of the dispicable mind control exercised by one deranged individual named James Warren Jones. We all have our strengths and weaknesses. Please accept what happened 20 years ago in Jonestown as a learning experience. Appreciate the strengths and forgive the weaknesses.

Jeff Brailey
San Antonio, Texas
September 18, 1998

APPENDIX

**AFFIDAVIT OF DEBORAH LAYTON BLAKEY
RE THE THREAT AND POSSIBILITY
OF MASS SUICIDE
BY MEMBERS OF THE PEOPLE'S TEMPLE**

I, DEBORAH LAYTON BLAKEY, declare the following under penalty of perjury:

1. The purpose of this affidavit is to call to the attention of the United States government the existence of a situation which threatens the lives of United States citizens living in Jonestown, Guyana.

2. From August, 1971 until May 13, 1978, I was a member of the People's Temple. For a substantial period of time prior to my departure for Guyana in December, 1977, I held the position of Financial Secretary of the People's Temple.

3. I was 18 years old when I joined the People's Temple. I had grown up in affluent circumstances in the permissive atmosphere of Berkeley, California. By joining the People's temple, I hoped to help others and in the process to bring structure and self-discipline into my own life.

4. During the years I was a member of the People's Temple, I watched the organization depart with increasing frequency from its professed dedication for social change and participatory democracy. The Rev. Jim Jones gradually assumed a tyrannical hold over the lives of Temple members.

5. Any disagreement with his dictates came to be regarded as "treason." The Rev. Jones labeled any person who left the organization a "traitor" and "fair game." He steadfastly and convincingly maintained that the punishment for defection was death. The fact that severe corporal punishment was frequently administered to Temple members gave the threats a frightening air of reality.

6. The Rev. Jones saw himself as the center of a conspiracy. The identity of the conspirators changed from day to day along with his erratic world vision. He induced the fear in others that, through their contact with him, they had become targets of the conspiracy. He convinced black Temple members that if they did not follow him to Guyana, they would be put into concentration camps and killed. White members were instilled with the belief that their names appeared on a secret list of enemies of the state that was kept by the C.I.A. and that they would be tracked down, tortured, imprisoned, and subsequently killed if they did not flee to Guyana.

7. Frequently, at Temple meetings, Rev. Jim Jones would talk non-stop for hours. At various times, he claimed that he was the reincarnation of either Lenin, Jesus Christ, or one of a variety of other religious or political figures. He claimed that he had divine powers and could heal the sick. He stated that he had extrasensory perception and could tell what everyone was thinking. He said that he had powerful connections the world over, including the Mafia, Idi Amin and the Soviet government.

8. When I first joined the Temple, Rev. Jones seemed to make clear distinctions between fantasy and reality. I believed that most of the time when he said irrational things, he was aware that they were irrational, but that they served as a tool of his leadership. His theory was that the end justifies the means. At other times, he appeared to be deluded by a paranoid vision of the world. He would not sleep for days at a time and talk compulsively about the conspiracies against him. However, as time went on, he appeared to become genuinely irrational.

9. Rev. Jones insisted that Temple members work long hours and completely give up all semblance of a personal life. Proof of loyalty to Jones was confirmed by actions showing that a member had given up everything, even basic necessities. The most loyal were in the worst

physical condition. Dark circles under one's eyes or extreme loss of weight were considered signs of loyalty.

10. The primary emotions I came to experience were exhaustion and fear. I knew that Rev. Jones was in some sense "sick," but that did not make me any less afraid of him.

11. Rev. Jones fled the United States in June, 1977 amidst growing public criticism of the practices of the Temple. He informed members of the Temple that he would be imprisoned for life if he did not leave immediately.

12. Between June, 1977 and December 1977, when I was ordered to depart from Guyana, I had access to coded radio broadcasts from Rev. Jones in Guyana to the People's Temple headquarters in San Francisco.

13. In September, 1977, an event which Rev. Jones viewed as a major crisis occurred. Through listening to coded radio broadcasts and conversations with other members of the Temple staff, I learned that an attorney for former Temple member Grace Stoen had arrived in Guyana, seeking the return of her son, John Victor Stoen.

14. Rev. Jones has expressed particular bitterness toward Grace Stoen. She had been Chief Counselor, a position of great responsibility within the Temple. Her personal qualities of generosity and compassion made her very popular with the membership. Her departure posed a threat to rev. Jones' absolute control. Rev. Jones delivered a number of public tirades against her. He said that her kindness was faked and that she was a C.I.A. agent. He swore that he would never return her son to her.

15. I am informed that Rev. Jones believed that he would be able to stop Timothy Stoen, husband of Grace Stoen and father of John Victor Stoen, from speaking against the Temple as long as the child was being held in Guyana. Timothy Stoen, a former Assistant District Attorney in

Mendocino and San Francisco counties, had been one of Rev. Jones' most trusted advisors. It was rumored that Stoen was critical of the use of physical force and other forms of intimidation against Temple members. I am further informed that Rev. Jones believed that a public statement by Timothy Stoen would increase the tarnish on his public image.

16. When the Temple lost track of Timothy Stoen, I was assigned to track him down and offer him a large sum of money in return for his silence. Initially, I was to offer him $5,000. I was authorized to pay him up to $10,000. I was not able to locate him and did not see him again until on or about October 6, 1977. On that date, the Temple received information that he would be joining Grace in a San Francisco Superior Court action to determine the custody of John. I was one of the group of Temple members assigned to meet him outside the court and attempt to intimidate him to prevent him from going inside.

17. The September, 1977 crisis concerning John Stoen reached major proportions. The radio messages from Guyana were frenzied and hysterical. One morning, terry J. Buford, public relations advisor to Rev. Jones, and myself were instructed to place a telephone call to a high-ranking Guyanese official who was visiting the United States and deliver the following threat: unless the government of Guyana took immediate steps to stall the Guyanese court action regarding John Stoen's custody, the entire population of Jonestown would extinguish itself in a mass suicide by 5:30 P.M. that day. I was later informed that Temple members in Guyana placed similar calls to other Guyanese officials.

18. We later received radio communication to the effect that the court case had been stalled and the suicide threat was called off.

19. I arrived in Guyana in December, 1977. I spent a week in Georgetown and then, pursuant to orders, traveled to Jonestown.

20. Conditions at Jonestown were even worse than I had feared they would be. The settlement was swarming with armed guards. No one was permitted to leave unless on a special assignment and these assignments were only given to the most trusted. We were allowed to associate with Guyanese people only while on a "mission."

21. The vast majority of the Temple members were required to work in the fields from 7 A.M. to 6 P.M. six days per week and on Sunday from 7 A.M. to 2 P.M. We were allowed one hour for lunch. Most of this hour was spent walking back to lunch and standing in line for our food. Taking any other breaks during the workday was severely frowned upon.

22. The food was woefully inadequate. There was rice for breakfast, rice water soup for lunch, and rice and beans for dinner. On Sunday, we each received an egg and a cookie. Two or three times a week we had vegetables. Some very weak and elderly members received one egg per day. However, the food did improve markedly on the few occasions when there were outside visitors.

23. In contrast, rev. Jones, claiming problems with his blood sugar, dined separately and ate meat regularly. He had his own refrigerator which was stocked with food. The two women with whom he resided, Maria Katsaris and Carolyn Layton, and the two small boys who lived with him, Kimo Prokes and John Stoen, dined with the membership. However, they were in much better physical shape than everyone else since they were allowed to eat the food in Rev. Jones' refrigerator.

24. In February, 1978, conditions became so bad that half of Jonestown was ill with severe diarrhea and high fevers. I was seriously ill for two weeks. Like most of the other sick people, I was not given any nourishing foods to help recover. I was given water and a tea drink until I was well enough to return to the basic rice and beans diet.

25. As the former financial secretary, I was aware that the Temple received over $65,000 in Social Security checks per month. It made me angry to see that only a fraction of the income of the senior citizens in the care of the Temple was being used for their benefit. Some of the money was being used to build a settlement that would earn Rev. Jones a place in history with which he was so obsessed. The balance was being held in "reserve." Although I felt terrible about what was happening, I was afraid to say anything because I knew that anyone with a differing opinion gained the wrath of Jones and other members.

26. Rev. Jones' thoughts were made known to the population of Jonestown by means of broadcasts over the loudspeaker system. He broadcast an average of six hours per day. When the Reverend was particularly agitated, he would broadcast for hours on end. He would talk on and on while we worked in the fields or tried to sleep. In a addition to the daily broadcasts, there were marathon meetings six nights per week.

27. The tenor of the broadcasts revealed that rev. Jones' paranoia had reached an all-time high. He was irate at the light in which he was being portrayed by the media. He felt that as a consequence of having been ridiculed and maligned, he would be denied a place in history. His obsession with his place in history was maniacal. When pondering the loss of what he considered his rightful place in history, he would grow despondent and say all was lost.

28. Visitors were infrequently permitted access to Jonestown. The entire community was required to put on a performance when a visitor arrived. Before the visitor arrived, rev. Jones would instruct us on the image we were to project. The workday would be shortened. The food would be better. Sometimes there would be music and dancing. Aside from these performances, there was little joy or hope in any of our lives. An air of despondency prevailed.

29. There was constant talk of death. In the early days of the People's temple, general rhetoric about dying for principles was sometimes heard. In Jonestown, the concept of mass suicide for socialism arose. Because our lives were so wretched anyway and because we were so afraid to contradict Rev. Jones, the concept was not challenged.

30. An event which transpired shortly after I reached Jonestown convinced me that Rev. Jones had sufficient control over the minds of the residents that it would be possible for him to effect a mass suicide.

31. At least once a week, Rev. Jones would declare a "white night," or state of emergency. The entire population of Jonestown would be awakened by blaring sirens. Designated persons, approximately fifty in number, would arm themselves with rifles, move from cabin to cabin, and make certain that all members were responding. A mass meeting would ensue. Frequently during these crises, we would be told that the jungle was swarming with mercenaries and that death could be expected at any minute.

32. During one "white night," we were informed that our situation had become hopeless and that the only course of action open to us was a mass suicide for the glory of socialism. We were told that we would be tortured by mercenaries if we were taken alive. Everyone, including the children, was told to line up. As we passed through the line, we were given a small glass of red liquid to drink. We were told that the liquid contained poison and that we would die within 45 minutes. We all did as we were told. When the time came when we should have dropped dead, Rev. Jones explained that the poison was not real and that we had just been through a loyalty test. He warned us that the time was not far off when it would become necessary for us to die by our own hands.

33. Life in Jonestown was so miserable and the physical pain of

exhaustion was so great that this event was not traumatic for me. I had become indifferent as to whether I lived or died.

34. During another "white night." I watched Carolyn Layton, my former sister-in-law, give sleeping pills to two young children in her care, John Victor Stoen and Kimo Prokes, her own son. Carolyn said to me that Rev. Jones had told her that everyone was going to have to die that night. She said that she would probably have to shoot John and Kimo and that it would be easier for them if she did it while they were asleep.

35. In April, 1978, I was reassigned to Georgetown. I became determined to escape or die trying. I surreptitiously contacted my sister who wired me a plane ticket. After I received the ticket, I sought the assistance of the United States Embassy in arranging to leave Guyana. Rev. Jones had instructed us that he had a spy working in the United States Embassy and that he would know if anyone went to the embassy for help. For this reason, I was very fearful.

36. I am most grateful to the United States government and Richard McCoy and Daniel Weber; in particular for the assistance they gave me. However, the efforts made to investigate conditions in Jonestown are inadequate for the following reasons. The infrequent visits are always announced and arranged. Acting in fear for their lives, Temple members respond as they are told. The members appear to speak freely to American representatives, but in fact they are drilled thoroughly prior to each visit on what questions to expect and how to respond. Members are afraid of retaliation if they speak their true feelings in public.

37. On behalf of the population of Jonestown, I urge that the United States government take adequate steps to safeguard their rights. I believe that their lives are in danger.

I declare under penalty of perjury that the foregoing is true and correct,except as to those matters stated on information and belief and as to those I believe them to be true.

Executed this 15th day of June, 1978 at San Francisco, California.

(signed) Deborah Layton Blakey

JONESTOWN TRANSCRIPT

The following extracts were taken from the transcript of a tape of the final 43 minutes of Jonestown's final "White Night" on November 18, 1978.

Jones: I've tried my best to give you a good life. In spite of all that I've tried, a handful of our people, with their lies, have made our life impossible. There's no way to detach ourselves from what's happened today.

Not only are we in a compound situation; not only are there those who have left and committed the betrayal of the century; some have stolen children from others and they are in pursuit right now to kill them, because they stole their children. And we are sitting here waiting on a powder keg.

So, to sit here and wait for the catastrophe that's going to happen on that airplane -- it's going to be a catastrophe. It almost happened here. You can't steal people's children. You can't take off with people's children without expecting a violent reaction. And that's not so unfamiliar to us either, even if we -- even if we were Judeo-Christian -- if we weren't Communists. The world opinion suffers violence and the violent shall take it by force. If we can't live in peace, then let's die in peace. [Applause]

We've been so betrayed. We have been so terribly betrayed. [Music and singing] What's going to happen here in a matter of a few minutes is that one of those people on that plane is going to shoot the pilot -- I know that. I didn't plan it, but I know it is going to happen. They're gonna shoot the pilot and down comes that plane into the jungle. And we better not have any of our children left when it's over. Because they'll parachute in here on us.

I'm going to be just as plain as I know how to tell you. I've never lied to you. I have never lied to you. I know that's what's gonna happen. That's what he intends to do; and he will do it. He'll do it. What's with being so bewildered with many, many pressures on my brain seeing all people behave so treasonous -- there was just too much for me to put together. But I now know what he was telling me. And it'll happen. If the plane gets in the air even.

So my opinion is that you be kind to children, and be kind to seniors, and take the potion like they used to in ancient Greece, and step over quietly; because we are not committing suicide -- it's a revolutionary act. We can't go back; they won't leave us alone. They're now going back to tell more lies, which means more congressmen. And there's no way, no way we can survive.

Anybody. Anyone that has any dissenting opinion, please speak. Yes. You can have an opportunity, but if the children are left, we're going to have them butchered. We can make a strike, but we'll be striking out against people that we don't want to strike against. We'd like to get the people that caused this stuff; and some -- if some people here are prepared and know how to do that, to go in town and get Timothy Stoen, but there's no plane. There's no plane. You can't catch a plane in time.

He's responsible for it. He brought these people to us. He and Deanna Myrtle. The people in San Francisco will not -- not be idle. Or would they? They'll not take our death in vain, you know. Yes?

Woman: Is it too late for Russia?

Jones: At this point, it's too late for Russia. They killed. They started to kill. That's why it makes it too late for Russia. Otherwise I'd say yes, sir, you bet your life. But it's too late. I can't control these people. They're out there. They've gone with the guns. And it's too late. And once we kill anybody -- at least that's the way I've always -- I've always put my lot with you. If one of my people do something, that's me. And they say I don't have to take the blame for this -- but I don't live that way. They said, deliver up Ejar; we tried to get that man back here. Ejar, whose mothers' been lying on him, and trying to break up this family. And they've all agreed to kill us by any means necessary. Do you think I'm going to deliver them Ejar? Not on your life.

Man: I know a way to find Stoen if it'll help us.

Jones: No. You're not going. You're not going. I can't live that way. I cannot live that way. I've lived with -- for all. I'll die for all. [Applause]

I've been living on hope for a long time, Christine, and I appreciate -- you've always been a very good agitator. I like agitation because you have to see two sides of one issue -- two sides of a question. But what those people are gonna get done; and what they get through will make our lives worse than hell. Will make us -- will make the rest of us not accept it. When they get through lying. They posed so many lies between there and that truck that we are -- we are done in as far as any other alternative.

Woman: Well, I say let's make an airlift to Russia. That's what I say. I don't think nothing is impossible, if you believe it.

Jones: How are we going to do that? How are you going to airlift to Russia?

Woman: Well, I thought they said if we got in an emergency, they gave you a code to let them know.

Jones: No, they didn't. They gave us a code that they'd let us know on that issue; not us create an issue for them. They said that we -- if they saw the country coming down, they'd give us a code. They'd give us a code. We can check on that and see if it's on the code. Did you check with Russia to see if they'll take us in a minute but otherwise we die?

I don't know what else to say to these people. But to me death is not a fearful thing. It's living that's cursed. I have never, never, never, never seen anything like this before in my life. I've never seen people take the law and do -- in their own hands and provoke us and try to purposely agitate mother of children. There is no need to finish us; it's not worth living like this. Not worth living like this.

Woman: I think that there were too few who left for 1,200 people to give them their lives for those people that left.

Jones: Do you know how many left?

Woman: Oh, twenty-odd. That's a small --

Jones: Some twenty-odd --

Woman: Compared to what's here.

Jones: Twenty-odd. But what's gonna happen when they don't leave? I hope that they could leave. But what's gonna happen when they don't leave?

Woman: You mean the people here?

Jones: Yeah. What's gonna happen to us when they don't leave, when they don't get on the plane and the plane goes down?

Woman: I don't think they'll go down.

Jones: You don't think they'll go down? I wish I could tell you was right -- but I'm right. There's one man who blames, and rightfully so, Judy Blakey for the murder -- for the murder of his mother and he'll -- he'll stop that pilot by any means necessary. He'll do it. That plane'll come out of the air. There's no way you can fly a plane without a pilot.

Woman: I wasn't speaking about that plane. I was speaking about a plane for us to go to Russia.

Jones: How -- to Russia? You think Russia's gonna want -- no -- you think Russia's gonna want us with all this stigma? We had some value, but now we don't have any value.

Woman: Well, I don't see it like that. I mean, I feel like that -- as long as there's life there's hope. That's my faith.

Jones: Well -- some -- everybody dies. Some place that hope runs out; because everybody dies. I haven't seen anybody yet didn't die. And I like to choose my own kind of death for a change. I'm tired of being tormented to hell, that's what I'm tired of. Tired of it. [Applause]

To have other people's lives in my hands, and I certainly don't want your life in my hands. I'm going to tell you Christine, without me, life has no meaning [Applause] I'm the best thing you ever had. I want -- want -- I have to pay -- I'm standing with [inaudible]. I'm standing with those people. They're part of me. I could detach myself. No. No. No. No. No. No. I never detach myself from any of your troubles. I've always taken your troubles right on my shoulders. And I'm not going to change that now. It's too late. I've been running too long. Not going to change now. [Applause]

Maybe the next time you'll get to go to Russia. The next time around. This is -- what I'm talking about now is the dispensation of judgement. This is a revolutionary -- a revolutionary suicide council. I'm not talking about self -- self -- destruction. I'm talking about what we have no other road. I will take your call. We will put it through to the Russians. And I can tell you the answer now, because I am a prophet. Call the Russians and tell them and see if they'll take us.

Woman: I said I'm not ready to die.

Jones: I don't think you are.

Woman: But I know what you meant.

Jones: I don't think you are.

Woman: But I look at all the babies and I think they deserve to live.

Jones: But don't they deserve much more -- they deserve peace.

Woman: We came here for peace.

Jones: And we've -- have we had it?

Woman: No.

Jones: I've tried to give it to you. I've laid down my life, practically. I've practically died every day to give you peace. And you still not have any peace. You look better than I've seen you in a long while but it's still not the kind of peace I want to give you.

Woman: I know that. But I still think, as an individual, I have a right to --

Jones: You do, and I'm listening.

Woman: -- to say what I think, what I feel. And think we all have the right to our own destiny as individuals.

Jones: Right.

Woman: And I think I have a right to choose mine and everybody has a right to choose theirs.

Jones: Yes. I'm not criticizing --

Woman: Well, I think I still have a right to my own opinion.

Jones: I'm not taking it from you. I'm not taking it from you.

Man: Christine, you're only standing here because he was here in the first place. So I don't know what you are talking about, having an individual life.

Your life has been extended to the day that you're standing there because of him.

Jones: I guess she has as much right to speak as anybody else to -- What did you say Ruby? [Voice cannot be deciphered] Well, you'll regret that, this very day if you don't die. You'll regret it if you do though you don't die. You'll regret it.

I saved them. I saved them, but I made my example. I made my expression. I made my manifestation and the world was ready, not ready for me. Paul said I was a man born out of due season. I've been born out of due season, just like all we are -- and the best testimony we can make is to leave this goddamn world [Applause]

Woman: You must prepare to die.

Woman: I'm not talking to her. Will you let -- would you let her or me talk?

Jones: Keep talking.

Woman: Would you make her sit down and let me talk while I'm on the floor or let her talk.

Jones: Flo, can you tell the leader what to do if you jive? I've listened to you. You asked me about Russia. I'm right now making a call to Russia. What more do you suggest? I'm listening to you. You've yet to give me one slight bit of encouragement. I just now... to go there and do that. [Voices]

Everybody hold it. We didn't come -- Hold it. Hold it. Hold it. [Voices]

Lay down your burden. I'm gonna lay down my burden. Down by the riverside. Shall we lay them down here by the side of Guyana? No man didn't take our lives. Right now. They haven't taken them. But when they start parachuting out of the air, they'll seek some of our innocent babies. I'm not -- I don't want... They've got to shoot me to get through to some of these people. I'm not telling them take your child. Can you let them take your child?

Voices: No. No. No.

Jones: I want to see... [Many voices] Please. Please. Please. Please. Please. Please. Please.

Man: I'm ready to go. If you tell us we have to give our lives now, we're ready -- all the rest of the sisters and brother are with me.

Jones: Some months I've tried to keep this thing from happening. But now I see it's the will -- it's the will of Sovereign Being that this happen to us. That we lay down our lives in protest against what's been done. The criminality of people. The cruelty of people.

Who walked out of here today? Do you know who walked out? [Voices] Mostly white people walked.

I'm so grateful for the ones that didn't -- those who knew who they are. I know there's no point -- there's no point to this. We are born before our time. They won't accept us. And I don't think we should sit here and take any more time for our children to be endangered. Because if they come after our children, we give them our children, then our children will suffer forever.

[Woman's voice - unintelligible]

Jones: What comes now, folks? What comes now?

Man: Everybody hold it.

Jones: Say peace. Say peace. Say peace. Say peace. What's come. Don't let -- Take Dwyer on down to the east house. Take Dwyer.

Woman: Everybody be quiet please.

Man: That means sit down. Sit down.

Jones: They know. I tried so very, very hard. They're trying over here to see what's going to happen in Los Angeles. Who is he?

[Voice]

Jones: Get Dwyer out of here before something happens to him. Dwyer. I'm not talking about Ejar. I said Dwyer. Ain't nobody gonna take Ejar. I'm not lettin' 'em take Ejar.

Woman: At one time, I felt just like [inaudible]... but after today I don't feel anything because the biggest majority of the people that left here for a fight and I know it really hurt my heart because --

Jones: Broke your heart, didn't it?

Woman: It broke my heart completely. All of this year the white people had been with us and they're not a part of us. So we might as well end it now, because I don't see -- [Music and voices]

Jones: Well, it's all over, all over. What a legacy, what a legacy. What's the Red Brigade doing, and one's that ever made any sense anyway. They invaded our privacy. They followed us 6,000 miles away. Red Brigade showed them justice. The congressman's dead.

Please get some medication. Simple. It's simple, there's no convulsions with it. It's just simple. Just, please, get it. Before it's too late. The G.D.F. will be here, I tell you. Get movin', get movin', get movin'.

[Voices]

Jones: Don't be afraid to die. You'll see people land out there. They'll torture some of our children here. They'll torture our people. They'll torture our seniors.

We cannot have this... Are you going to separate yourself from who shot the congressman. I don't know who shot him.

Voices: No. No. No.

Jones: Let's make our peace. And those had a right to go, and they had a right to -- how many are dead? Aw, God, Almighty God. Huh. Patty Park is dead?

[Voices]

Woman: Some of the others who are... long enough in a safe place to write about...

Jones: I don't know how in the world they are ever going to write about us. It's just too late. It's too late. The congressman's dead. The... Many of our... are dead. They all laying out there dead.

Please can we hasten? Can we hasten with our medication? You don't know what you've done. I tried. [Applause and music]

They saw it happen and ran into the bush and dropped the machine guns. Never in my life. But we've got to move. Are you gonna get that education here? You've got to move. Approximately about 40 minutes.

Woman: Do... have to know when the people that are standing in the aisles. Go stand in the radio room yard. Everybody get behind a table and back this way. OK. There's nothing to worry about. Everybody keep calm; and try to keep your children calm. And all those children that help, let the little children in and reassure them. They're not crying from pain. It's just a little bitter tasting. They're not crying from pain. Annie, Miguel, can I please see you back...

Man: So much to do before I came here. So let me tell you about it. It may make a lot of you feel a little more comfortable. Sit down and be quiet please.

One of the things I used to do -- I used to be a therapist. And the kind of therapy I did had to do with reincarnations in past life situations. And any time anybody had an experience of going into a past life, I was fortunate enough through Father to be able to let them experience it all the way through their death, so to speak. And everybody was so happy when they made that step to the other side.

Woman: I just want to say something for everyone that I see is standing around, or crying. This is nothing to cry about. This is something we all could rejoice about. We could be happy about this. They always told us that we could cry when you're coming into this world. So we are leaving it and we are leaving it peaceful. I think we should be -- you should be happy about this. I was just thinking about Jim Jones. He just has suffered and suffered and suffered. We have the honor guard and we don't even have a chance to... here... one more chance. That's few that's gone. There's many more here... That's not all of us. That's not all, yet. That's just a few that have died. I'm looking at so many people crying. I wish you would not cry. [Applause] I've been here one year and nine months. And I never felt better in my life. Not in San Francisco. But until I came to Jonestown. I had a... life. I had a beautiful life. We should be happy. At least I am [Applause]

[Music]

Woman: Good to be alive today. I just like to thank Dad 'cause he was the only one that stood up for me when I needed him. And thank you, Dad.

Woman: I'm glad you are my brothers and sisters. I'm glad to be here.

[Voices]

Jones: Please. Fir God's sake, let's get on with it. We lived -- we've lived as no other people lived and loved We've had as much of this world as you're gonna get. Let's just be done with it. Let's be done with the agony of it. [Applause]

It's far, far harder to have to walk through every day, die slowly -- and from the time you're a child till the time you get gray, you're dying.

Dishonest, and I'm sure that they'll -- they'll pay for it. This is a revolutionary suicide. This is not a self-destructive suicide. So they'll pay for this. They brought this upon us. And they'll pay for that. I leave that destiny to them.

[Voices]

Jones: -- wants to go with their child has a right to go with their child. I think it's humane. I want to go -- I want to see you go though. They can take me and do what they want -- whatever they want to do. I want to see you go. I don't want to see you go through this hell no more. No more. No more. No more.

We're trying. If everybody -- relax. The best thing you do to relax and you won't have no problem with this thing. If you just relax.

Man: -- a great deal because it's Jim Jones. And the way the children are laying there now. I'd rather see them lay like that than to see them have to die like the jews did, which was pitiful anyhow. And I just like to thank Dad, who gave them this life and also death. And I appreciate the fact that our children are going. Because, like Dad said, when they came in, what they're going to do to our children -- they're going to massacre our children. And also the ones they take capture, they're gonna just let them grow up and be dummies, just like they want them to be. And not grow up to be a person like the one and only Jim Jones. So I'd like to thank Dad for the opportunity for letting Jonestown be not what it could be, but what Jonestown is. Thank you Dad. [Applause]

Man: It is not to be feared. It is not to be feared. It is a friend. It's a friend sitting there. Show your love for one another. Take your time --

Jones: Let's get gone. Let's get gone. Let's get gone. We had nothing we could do. We can't separate ourselves from our own people. For twenty years lying in some old rotten nursing home. Taking us through all these anguish years. They took us and put us in chains and that's nothing. This business -- that business -- there's no comparison to that, to this. They've robbed us of our land and they've taken us and driven us and we tried to find ourselves. We tried to find a new beginning. But it is too late. You can't separate yourself from your brother and your sister. No way I'm going to do it. I refuse. I don't know who fired the shot. I don't know who killed the congressman. But as far as I'm concerned, I killed him. You understand what I am saying? I killed him. He had no business coming. I told him not to come.

Woman: Right. Right.

[Music] [Children crying]

Jones: I, with respect, die with the beginning of dignity. Lay down your life with dignity. Don't lay down with tears and agony. It's nothing to death. It's like Mac said, it's just stepping over to another plane. Don't be this way. Stop this hysterics. This is not the way for people who are socialists or communists to die. No way for us to die. We must die with some dignity... and we have no choice. Now we have some choice. Do you think they're gonna allow this to be done? And allow us to get by with this? You must be insane -- children, it's just something to put you to rest, oh God.

[Children crying]

Jones: Mother, mother, mother, mother, mother, please. Mother, please, please, please. Don't do this. Don't do this. Lay down your life with your child, but don't do this.

Free at last. Keep -- keep your emotions down. Keep your emotions down. Children, it will not hurt. If you'd be -- if you be quiet. If you be quiet.

[Music] [Children crying]

Jones: It's never been done before, you say. It's been done by every tribe in history. Every tribe facing annihilation. All the Indians of the Amazon are doing it right now. They refuse to bring any babies into the world. Because they don't want to live in this kind of a world.

So be patient. Be patient. Death is -- I tell you, I don't care how many screams you hear. I don't care how many anguished cries. Death is a million times more preferable to spend more days in this life. If you knew what was ahead of you -- if you knew what was ahead of you, you'd be glad to be stepping over tonight.

Death. Death. Death is common to people. And the Eskimos, they take death in their stride. Let's be digni -- let's be dignified. If you quit telling them they're dying -- if you would also stop some of this nonsense -- adults, adults, I call on you to stop this nonsense. I call on you to quit exciting your children, when all they're doing is going to a quiet rest. I call on you to stop this now, if you have any respect at all. Are we black, proud, socialist -- or what are we? Now stop this nonsense. Don't carry this on any more. You're exciting your children.

All over and it's good. No -- no sorrow that it's all over. I'm glad it's over. Hurry, hurry, my children. Hurry. All I -- the hands of the enemy. Hurry, my children. Hurry. There are seniors out there that I am concerned about.

Hurry. I don't want any of my seniors to this mess. Only quickly, quickly, quickly, quickly, quickly. Let's just -- Good knowing you.

No more pain, Al. No more pain, I said, Al. No more pain. Jim Cobb is laying on the airfield dead at this moment. [Applause] Remember, the Oliver woman said she -- she'd come over and kill me if her son wouldn't stop her. These, these are the people, the peddlers of hate. All we're doing is laying down our lives. We're not letting them take our lives. We're laying down our lives. Peace in their lives. They just want peace.

Man: I'd just like to say that my -- my so-called parents are filled with so much hate and treachery. I think you people out here should think about your relatives were and be glad that the children are being laid to rest. And I'd like to thank Dad for making me strong to stand with it all and make me ready for it. Thank you.

Jones: All they do is taking a drink. They take it to go to sleep. That's what death is, sleep -- I'm tired of it all.

Woman: Everything we could have ever done, most loving thing of all of us could have done and it's been a pleasure walking with all of you in this revolutionary struggle. No other way I would rather go than to give my life for socialism, communism. And I thank Dad very, very much.

Woman: Dad's love and nursing, goodness and kindness and bring us to this land of freedom. His love -- his mother was the advance -- the advance guard to socialism. And his love, his nurses will go on forever unto the fields of --

Jones: - - to that, to that, to that, words to that -- was the green scene thing.

Woman: Go on unto the sign. And thank you Dad.

Jones: With the green -- and please bring it here so the adults can begin. --

you don't, don't fail to follow my advice. You'll be sorry. You'll be sorry.

We do it, then they do it. Have trust. You have to step across. We used to think this world was -- this world was not our home, and it sure isn't -- saying, it sure wasn't.

-- don't want to tell them. All he's doing -- if they will tell them -- assure these -- can't some people assure these children of the -- in stepping over to the next plane. They set an example for others. We said -- one thousand people who said, we don't like the world the way it is. Take our life from us. We laid it down. We got tired. We didn't commit suicide, we committed an act of revolutionary suicide protesting the conditions of an inhumane world.

[Organ music]

"Last Rights"

By Rebecca Moore

The following excerpted essay first appeared **In Defense of Peoples Temple - And Other Essays,** by Rebecca Moore (Lewiston NY: Edwin Mellon Press, 1988). It describes how the bodies of Jonestown victims were mishandled by various governmental agencies; and it details how family members of victims were treated by those agencies. The author appreciates Ms. Moore's permission to include this important excerpt in his book. It tells the rest of the story of the ghosts of November.

If you're a cultist, you don't have the same civil rights ordinary Americans enjoy. If you die, the government doesn't have to perform an autopsy, or investigate your death. It can entertain the notion of dumping you into a mass grave. It can destroy evidence of the cause of your death, frustrate your family's efforts to secure your remains, stick you in an airport hangar on a military base 3000 miles from home for weeks on end, and depend upon public apathy to get away with it.

This is exactly what happened to the people who died in Jonestown. In spite of the shock waves that rippled around the world from the jungle community in Guyana, the U.S. government failed to determine precisely how the people in Jonestown died. The Carter Administration characterized the suicides as an aberration lacking relevance to American society. As a result, the government agencies responsible for handling the bodies resolved the problems they presented by ignoring routine investigative procedures. They simply abandoned civilized treatment of the dead.

The people of Jonestown were treated as so many pieces of meat. They were dumped in bags, shipped to a place in the U.S. far from most relatives, embalmed, frozen until a non-governmental organization forced a court in San Francisco to pay for internment, and forgotten. Although 900 people died, only seven were autopsied. Two of the seven were my sisters.

The official attitude towards these cultists pervaded American society as well. Few questioned the hands-off policy taken by the State Department, the Justice Department, and the state of Delaware, where the bodies were warehoused over the Christmas holidays of 1978. Only a handful of forensic pathologists challenged the assault on our sense of justice implicit in the failure to perform meaningful postmortem examinations. "This was not garbage to be picked up," said Cyril Wecht, the medical examiner for Allegheny County, Pennsylvania.

> It shouldn't matter what we thought of cults or whether these people deserved to die. There should be no moral, ethical or philosophical decisions. We should behave like a responsible country or agency.

Perhaps the magnitude of the tragedy explains why the government mishandled what was essentially a criminal investigation. Nine hundred people don't commit suicide *en masse* every day . In a philosophical sense, Jonestown was a cataclysmic event that raised unanswerable questions about the human spirit. In a more mundane sense, however, it was simply a case of 900 suspicious deaths.

For our family, concerns centered on the deaths of Carolyn, Annie, and Carolyn's son Kimo, as well as many other people we knew and liked. Despite the shock during the first week of indescribable horror, we still wanted to know exactly how they died: in what manner and form, and when and where. The very few eyewitness accounts were contradictory, and said little about our relatives.

Our concern took on a note of uneasiness when newspapers reported that Annie had been found in the Temple leader Jim Jones' cabin, half her head blown away by a gunshot wound. Out of 900 people, only two were shot: Jim Jones and Annie Moore. We wanted to know what distinguished those two deaths from all the others.

In addition, news accounts reported the existence of a Peoples Temple hit squad. Several ex-members named my sister Carolyn as a leader of such a squad and voiced suspicion that she was not really dead.

Autopsies seemed imperative. With a lot of bad press about Peoples temple in general, and about Carolyn in particular, we felt we had to establish records about their deaths while we had the chance. If something were to come up later, we would have no protection against possible legal actions. A misidentification could have repercussions we could barely imagine, What if, for example, Annie had not been shot? What if the rumors of Carolyn's survival persisted? We had to be sure we had the right bodies, with manner and means of death legally confirmed. The U.S. government did not make it easy. Persuading the Justice Department to perform autopsies on my sisters proved time-consuming, exhausting and demoralizing. Getting the State Department and Delaware to release the bodies turned out to be another problem. Everyone who had realties to bury faced the same situation: unimaginable insensitivity and arrogance.

"When anyone dies by violence, or suspicion of violence," wrote the late Dr. Milton Helper, chief medical examiner of New York City, "regardless of whether violence is suicidal, accidental, or undetermined, it is an ancient responsibility of government to officially inquire into the death. This is of paramount importance to the administration of justice."

Quite simply, our government did not do justice to the people who died in Jonestown. By failing to take on the "ancient responsibility" of investigating the deaths of its citizens, our government denied some people -- mostly black, mostly poor, mostly idealistic -- due process. Our government said it was doing us a big favor by giving my sisters autopsies. But after the "big favor," we still didn't know how they died.

Dr. Leslie Mootoo, Guyana's chief pathologist, along with an American forensic pathologist sent by the Defense Department, performed brief examinations on Congressman Ryan and the others who died at the airstrip. Mootoo also visually examined over 200 bodies in Jonestown. He later told a Guyana coroner's jury that he saw needle marks on at least 70. With the help of American pathologist Dr. Lynn Crook, Mootoo concluded that cyanide was present in some of the bodies. An analysis of the contents of the vat revealed several tranquilizers as well as two strong poisons: potassium cyanide and potassium chloride.

While the Guyana Defense Force searched the jungle for survivors November 19th, Assistant Police Commissioner Skip Roberts and Jonestown survivor Odell Rhodes attached cardboard tags to 183 bodies Rhodes could identify by name. He recognized many, but frequently knew only a nickname or first name. Other survivors who came to help were stunned, and unable to assist.

Guyana waived its requirement for autopsies in the case of unnatural death, to expedite removal of the corpses. Some American pathologists blamed the lack of adequate on-site examination of the bodies on Guyana's haste to be rid of them. Dr. William Cowan, deputy director of the Armed Forces Institute of Pathology, said "the Government of Guyana just wanted the bodies out of there." He felt the government was extremely hostile. Dr. Lynn Crook said Guyana police allowed him to look at the bodies, but not to touch anything.

However, Guyana cannot be held totally responsible for the American failure to take field samples. Col. William Gordon, who was in charge of the body recovery operation, said he wasn't aware of the importance of postmortem examinations. "I don't know of any discussions that took place... No one mentioned it tome as being critical or necessary."

The confusion and antagonism among federal agencies rivaled that between the U.S. and Guyana. The State Department, the Defense Department, the Justice Department and the Office of Management and Budget eventually established a Federal Task Force to coordinate activities. State organized the Task Force since American deaths occurring outside the U.S. comes under its jurisdiction. It supervised the whole operation and took charge of notifying kin and releasing bodies. The Defense Department handled logistics: body removal, clean-up and storage. The Armed Forces Institute of Pathology, along with the FBI, worked on identification. The Justice Department investigated Ryan's death under a statute which makes it a federal crime to assassinate a Member of Congress anywhere in the world. It also went after Temple assets to reimburse the government for the cost of recovering the bodies. OMB monitored the cost of the airlift and subsequent identification.

The division of labor immediately created jurisdictional problems. For that reason we never learned exactly who made the decision to send the bodies to Dover Air Force Base in Delaware, although perhaps the State and Defense Departments collaborated on that as well. We were puzzled that the Air Force didn't take the victims to Oakland Army Base in California, site of a large military mortuary which had processed bodies during the Vietnam War. Most of the victims' families lived in California, where Peoples Temple was headquartered. It would have been easy to request, and obtain, medical records, especially from San Francisco. Finally, the bodies would not have had to been shipped across country for burial, an impossible expense for many relatives. Moving the bodies from one distant place to another -- Guyana to Delaware -- continued to alienate relatives from their dead.

Newspapers and officials gave two reasons for taking the bodies to Dover. First, it was closer to Guyana. Transporting them to Oakland, or to Travis Air Force Base fifty miles north, would have required the planes to stop en route for refueling. Second, the Dover mortuary was supposed to be better equipped to handle a large number of dead people. A few years earlier it had processed 327 bodies of Americans killed in an air crash at Tenerife, Canary Islands.

As it turned out, the Dover mortuary could not handle the Jonestown job by itself. Volunteers from the air base supplemented the mortuary's small full-time staff. Thirty-five pathologists and specialists from Walter Reed Hospital in Washington, D.C., 29 graves registration experts from Fort Lee, Virginia, and FBI fingerprint technicians also worked on the remains. Additionally, a local funeral director who had an annual contract with the mortuary received about a quarter million dollars for his participation in the processing. He charged the federal government $413 for each adult and $232 for each child.

The government's stated reasons for choosing Delaware are totally fabricated, since most of the people working on the Jonestown bodies did not normally work at the Dover mortuary. The volunteers and specialists could have worked anywhere.

We believe the bodies went to Dover simply because they would be close to government bureaucrats in Washington, D.C. who might have to travel there. We also believe the Air Force flew the victims to Delaware rather than California because the government didn't want to be hassled by relatives. NBC Nightly News reported that Dover was selected because of its "distance from California, thus reducing chances of families crowding the scene."

As far as we were concerned, dumping the bodies at Dover -- 3000 miles from the Temple's headquarters -- demonstrated extreme callousness on the part of the U.S. government. Coupled with the State Department's desire to bury everyone in Guyana, we felt the government forgot that the bodies had once been people, with kin who still owed them.

People in San Francisco and California were more sympathetic than the people in Delaware. The Temple was a California institution. Unlike Delaware, the San Francisco bay area has a large black population. If the move to Delaware was calculated to dilute sympathy for the victims, it worked.

Early Thursday morning, November 23, the first bodies arrived in Dover. That same day, the mortuary staff announced that all bodies would be cleaned and embalmed. But they were not routinely embalmed at first according to Dr. Cowan. The Armed Forces Institute of Pathology apparently hesitated two or three days while the Justice and State Departments haggled over the question of autopsies. With no resolution to the issue imminent, AFIP then decided to proceed with the embalming.

New York Times reports corroborate this time frame. The **Times** noted that five bodies were embalmed on Friday, November 24. By the following Monday, Dover morticians had embalmed only 70 bodies. Since all the bodies had arrived by then, they were not automatically embalmed. However, a news article on Wednesday, November 29, reported that after all the bodies were fingerprinted, embalming would begin "in earnest."

AFIP's decision to embalm -- replacing body fluids with a preservative -- was critical. It precluded and meaningful postmortem examinations by destroying physical evidence within the bodies. The pathologists knew that when they made the decision. Which means someone consciously decided that there would be no autopsies. Although AFIP could have saved the fluids for later testing, it didn't. "We didn't have any authority," Dr. Cowan claimed four months after the fact.

Morticians at the air base justified the embalming because it arrested decomposition and allowed the FBI to fingerprint and identify the remains. One mortician told us, our main concern was to preserve the bodies. The rationale rings false, though. By Saturday night, FBI identification experts had taken fingerprints from 374 bodies. Few of them had been embalmed.

With or without the embalming, identification proved to be a difficult task. The names Odell Rhodes and Skip Roberts carefully wrote on cardboard tags, had washed off in the rain and humidity. People in Jonestown wore each others' clothes, so the name tags sewn into collars and waist bands were of no help. One man wore the clothes of several different people. None, it turned out, were his own. The kerosene used to kill maggots made it difficult to get good fingerprints.

The State Department was supposed to help in getting records and then, once a positive identification was made, to notify the next of kin. It publicly requested medical and dental records from the relatives. We noticed the request by chance in a two-paragraph article buried in the **San Francisco Chronicle.** ABC News announced a phone number which State had provided for information -- and displayed a different number on the screen during the announcement. It's amazing the Air Force got as many as 100 records by December 1, considering how little the State Department did to help.

Dental and fingerprint records also arrived from Guyana by the first of December. Over 700 adults had been fingerprinted upon entering the country, and the records helped the stalled identification process. According to the FBI, it would have been impossible to identify more than 100 victims without Guyana's records.

Morticians from Dover, AFIP pathologists, the FBI, and air base volunteers worked around the clock in eight-hour shifts, printing, x-raying, cleaning and embalming the bodies. Wearing blue baseball caps with white FBI letters on them, the workers looked like a baseball team, according to one report.

Two and a half weeks after the deaths, the workers had positively identified 521 bodies. The remains, bagged and kept in refrigerated trucks until processing, were placed in caskets and stored in Bays 3, 4, and 5 at the Air Force base. All information about an individual was keyed to the number assigned in Jonestown.

Army volunteers had numbered the bodies in no apparent order. Ann was number A001, while Carolyn was number 2A. They lay ten feet apart in Jones' cabin. Skip Roberts claimed the Army assigned numbers one through 22 to bodies found in outlying houses. He believed the first thirteen referred to bodies in Jones' cabin. However, Dr. Cowan told us a woman found in Jones' cabin was numbered in the "B" series.

In theory, Carolyn's son, Kimo should have been among the first thirteen counted. Several news articles quoted individuals who saw him there alive while the suicides were in progress. We believe Odell Rhodes identified Kimo and another child in the cabin, since the first bodylift included Jones and two children he was believed to have fathered, according to the **Washington Post.** We knew Kimo was Jones' son before he was born.

Roberts told us there were three children in Jones' cabin, two boys on bunk beds and an infant lying between a couple on Jones' bed. We could see the two boys in a photograph Roberts showed us, and he pointed out John Victor Stoen, a child Jim Jones claimed to have sired. Dr. Cowan implied he knew the other boy was Kimo, but the Armed Forces Institute of Pathology failed to give either of the boys a positive identification.

Carolyn was one of the first people to be identified, ten days after the deaths. The State Department gave out the phone numbers of Dover morticians at random. After several phone calls and a late night trip to Dover, 120 miles from our home in Washington, we contracted the services of the Minus Funeral Home. The owner and his wife were like many members of the Temple itself: concerned, friendly and black. They listened to us explain our need for autopsies and agreed to help us find a pathologist somewhere in the state who would perform them. The Justice Department had already announced it was not going to authorize autopsies.

Two days later, Justice reversed its decision -- at least partially -- and announced it would autopsy Jim Jones, Maria Katsaris, Larry Schact, and four randomly selected bodies. We also heard the Air Force would perform autopsies on request, so my parents sent a telegram authorizing examinations for Carolyn and Ann. We also called Justice to see what its autopsy policy was.

Mike Abbell, head of the Criminal Division of the Justice Department, told reporters that public criticism prompted the agency to reconsider its earlier decision not to perform any autopsies.

> We're better off to put things to rest at an early date and make sure that all questions are reasonably answered rather than face second guesses in ten to fifteen years... We thought a full pathological investigation, at least of selected individuals, would be desirable to put the questions to rest.

Abbell's announcement was a bit more modest than that of Assistant Attorney General Philip Heyman, who declared that the Justice Department intended to "find out exactly how and why more than 900 Americans died in the jungle of Guyana."

The state's eagerness to get rid of the Jonestown victims created a merry-go-round of confusion which ultimately delayed the release of the bodies. In the beginning Governor Pierre DuPont's press aide announced Delaware's policy this way: "Claimed and identified bodies, for which there are requests to bury them in Delaware, cannot be removed from the Air Force Base in the absence of death certificates." But neither the state's attorney general nor the medical examiner would issue death certificates. Next, Delaware funeral directors could remove bodies from the air base only by a signed statement swearing they would transport the remains out of state. But the funeral homes we contacted in Washington, D.C. said they could not perform cremations without death certificates. Which brought us back to the beginning.

Delaware prevailed because the State Department could not cope with the situation. Although responsible for overseeing this part of the bodylift, State's lack of coordination led to missed and contradictory communications. For example, we called the State Department liaison in Dover to find out if Carolyn and Ann had been embalmed, since we learned it would adversely affect the autopsies. The liaison, Mike White, told us to call the base mortuary.

The mortuary told us to call Mike White. We went back and forth several times before we finally learned from the mortuary that my sisters had been embalmed.

The State Department could have ordered the mortuary to retain blood and urine samples for future analysis. State could have kept the bodies on ice for several weeks. But the State Department would not act. It viewed Jonestown as a political, rather than criminal case. The suicides were an international embarrassment. Better to leave the bodies in Guyana, or dump them in a mass grave in Delaware, or get rid of them quickly somehow, than think of them as people.

State defended its conduct by asserting it had no authority to investigate deaths of U.S. citizens in foreign countries. But it wouldn't tell us who did have authority. In fact, no one from any state or federal governmental agency we spoke with ever admitted anything but the most limited responsibility. When the Justice Department finally decided to authorize autopsies, in response to public criticism, it was too late for the examinations to be meaningful.

On December 15, almost a month after the suicides, AFIP examined the remains of Carolyn and Ann, as well as Jim Jones, Dr. Larry Schact, Maria Katsaris, Richard Castillo and Violet Dillard. Our family and Dr. Schact's were the only two to request the examinations. A few days later, we learned that the Air Force had allowed Dr. Rudiger Breitenecker, a Baltimore forensic pathologist, to witness the proceedings. It was an ironic twist, since Dr. Breitenecker was the independent pathologist we wanted to be present in the first place.

Breitenecker told the **New York Times** that Jones and Annie had died of gunshot wounds to the head, consistent with either suicide or murder. In Jones' case, however, the contact wound made him a likely suicide. Breitenecker felt the cause of death of the other five people might never be known because of advanced decomposition and embalming.

Our arduous efforts to obtain autopsies and our four-month wait produced inconclusive results. For Annie:

> Cause of Death: Acute cyanide poisoning; gunshot wound
> of the head, laceration of the brain.
> Manner of Death: Undetermined.

For Carolyn:

Cause of Death: Probable cyanide poisoning.
Manner of Death: Undetermined.

Grisly details filled the reports: maggots; fingers amputated to obtain prints and then tossed back into the body bag; decomposition making them unrecognizable; incisions made to compare teeth with dental records; and of course, the horror of Ann's mutilation by gunshot wound. We dealt with these horrors by compartmentalizing them. They had nothing to do with the persons we knew as Carolyn and Ann. The autopsies were scientific procedures performed on human flesh, not human beings.

Kimo, like 234 other children, was never identified. The photos we sent to the FBI were of no use.

Metal coffins containing the bodies of unidentified, and some identified but unclaimed victims, were stacked at Dover Air Force Base. They sat there while the State Department pondered a decision. On January 19, 1979, the day we buried Carolyn and Ann in California, State suggested dumping the remaining bodies in West Virginia.

Delaware had already refused to accept the bodies, although State Senator W. Lee Littleton offered to bury 30 to 40 Peoples Temple children in his backyard so he could "watch their bodies rise on Judgement Day." In December, Governor Pierre DuPont asked President Carter to fly the bodies to California, but the State Department insisted the government had neither the authority nor the money to release the bodies.

Religious workers and churches in San Francisco had been talking and working together on the Peoples Temple problem since November 19. In December, the ad hoc group called the Emergency Relief Committee, urged the courts to set aside one million dollars of Temple assets for burial costs.

On March 30, 1979, a San Francisco Superior Court judge awarded the committee $300,000 out of Temple assets to pay for the operation. It was another month, though, before the bodies left Delaware. The problem was a lack of destination. Various communities in California resisted the idea of having a mass grave in neighboring cemeteries.

Skyline Memorial Park in San Mateo originally agreed to accept the bodies at a cost of $349.10 for a single interment, and $560.70 for double depth interment in the same space. The cemetery backed out after nearby residents complained. Marin County's Daphne Fernwood Cemetery was willing to bury the remains, but the Marin County Board of Supervisors adopted a resolution asking the bodies be interred in several counties. Finally, Evergreen Cemetery, located in a predominantly black neighborhood near Mills College in Oakland, accepted the bodies.

In late April 1979, the bodies finally made it to the West Coast, transported on tractor-trailers by a Delaware moving company. One hundred identified remains went to Fort McArthur in Los Angeles, while another 201 went to Oakland Army Base. The 234 bodies which were still unidentified -- mostly of children -- went directly to Evergreen Cemetery. After months of organizing, including filing a lawsuit, the Emergency relief Committee anticipated that many relatives would come forward.

"The reaction was just the opposite of what we expected," Donetter Lane, the president of the San Francisco Council of Churches, told us. "We expected a lot of calls, lots of interest. We'd been working on this a long time. But when the bodies arrived, nothing. No response."

One reason the committee wasn't flooded with calls was a court order that required relatives to file a statement of destitution before any bodies could be released to them. This discouraged many who were not poor, but could not afford the extraordinary costs associated with moving bodies across country and burying them. The fact that many lost more than one relative added to the burden.

Evergreen Cemetery buried the unclaimed and unidentified in a mass grave on a steeply sloping hillside. It was May 11, 1979, almost six months after they died. Kimo, we believe, is buried there.

At the end of November 1978, the federal government claimed its Jonestown expenses ran to $9 million. When the Justice Department finally filed a civil suit against Peoples Temple in January 1979, the figure shrank by half, to $4.3 million. And in May 1979, the General Accounting Office calculated a cost of $4800 per body, or close to $4.4 million for the entire operation.

This doesn't seem like too much to spend on "the proper and decent thing to do," White House Press Secretary Jody Powell said of the airlift. In fact, the government could have done much more for the people who died in Jonestown. It could have followed routine forensic procedures to accurately determine how 900 people actually met their deaths.

The United States government wronged the victims of Jonestown and their families when it removed the bodies from Guyana without making any tests at the scene of the crime. It wronged them, and us, when it took the bodies to Dover, Delaware. It wronged us when it embalmed the bodies before conducting postmortem examinations.

By failing to follow routine medico-legal procedures, the government raised questions about its own performance and motives regarding Peoples Temple. More important, however, it obscured the true cause of the deaths in Jonestown, irrevocably.

Recommended Reading

David Chidester, *Salvation and Suicide: An Interpretation of the Peoples Temple and Jonestown* Bloomington: Indiana University, 1988

John R. Hall, *Gone from the Promised Land: Jonestown in American Cultural History* New Brunswick, NJ: Transaction Books, 1987

Laurie Efrein Kahalas, *Snake Dance: Unravelling the Mysteries of Jonestown,* Vancouver: Trafford Publishing, 1998

Mary McCormick Maaga, *Hearing Voices of Jonestown,* Syracuse: Syracuse University Press, 1998

Rebecca Moore, *A Sympathetic History of Jonestown,* Lewiston, NY: Edwin Mellon Press, 1985

ibid, *The Jonestown Letters: Correspondence of the Moore Family 1970-1985,* Lewiston, Edwin Mellon Press, 1985

ibid, *In Defense of Peoples Temple,* Lewiston, NY: Edwin Mellon Press, 1989

Rebecca Moore and Fielding McGehee, III, editors *New Religious Movements, Mass Suicide, and Peoples Temple: Scholarly Perspectives on a Tragedy,* Lewiston, NY: Edwin Mellon Press, 1989

ibid, *The Need for a Second Look at Jonestown,* Lewiston, NY: Edwin Mellon Press, 1989

Tim Reiterman and John Jacobs, *Raven: The Untold Story of the Rev. Jim Jones and His People,* New York: Dutton, 1982

Steve Rose, *jesus and Jim Jones: Behind Jonestown,* New York: The Pilgrim Press, 1979

Judith Weightman, *Making Sense of the Jonestown Suicides,* Lewiston, NY: The Edwin Mellon Press, 1983

ORDER FORM

FAX ORDER (210) 641-5192

TELEPHONE ORDER (888) 82 GHOST

POSTAL ORDER J & J Publications
P.O. Box 240808
San Antonio, TX 78224

Please send me _____ copies of THE GHOSTS OF NOVEMBER: Memoirs of an Outsider Who Witnessed the Carnage at Jonestown, Guyana. I understand that I may return any books for a full refund -- for any reason, no questions asked.

Name: ______________________________

Address: ______________________________

City: ____________________ State ____ Zip: __________

Telephone: (   ) ______________________

Book Prices

1 book	$19.95ea
2-5	18.95ea
6-10	17.95ea
11-15	15.95ea
16-20	13.95ea
21-25	11.95ea
26+	9.95ea

Sales Tax: Please add 7.75% for books shipped to Texas.

Shipping: $4.00 for the first book & 2.00 more for each additional book.

Order Now Toll Free
THANKS FOR YOUR ORDER!!

Payment

☐ Cheque

☐ Credit Card ☐ VISA ☐ MasterCard ☐ Discover

Card Number: ____________________ Exp Date: ____/____

Name on Card: ______________________________